TERMS OF ADORNMENT

t TERMS OF ADORNMENT

accessories

Deborah Chase

drawings by Carleen Powell

HarperCollins*Publishers*

The artwork on pages 29, 56, 57, 86, 94, 98, 104, 106, 107, 148, 158, 194, and 211 appears courtesy of Macy's Department Store.

The artwork on pages 26, 186, and 223 appears courtesy of Sears, Roebuck and Co.

HarperCollins books may be purchased for
educational, business, or sales promotional use.
For information please write:
Special Markets Department,
HarperCollins Publishers, Inc.,
10 East 53rd Street, New York, NY 10022.

FIRST EDITION

Designed by BTDnyc

LIBRARY OF CONGRESS CATALOGING-IN-PUBLICATION DATA
Chase, Deborah.
    Terms of adornment : the ultimate guide to accessories / by Deborah Chase. — 1st ed.
      p.   cm.
    Includes index.
    ISBN 0–06–273454–7
    1. Dress accessories. 2. Fashion. I. Title.
    TT560.C47 1998   98–12710
    646'.34—dc21   CIP

99 00 01 02 03 ❖/RRD 1 2 3 4 5 6 7 8 9 10

CONTENTS

MY LADY'S GLOVE

Acknowledgments

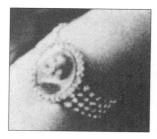

A book is more than words on paper, much more. It consists of the dozens of people who generously contribute their time, experience, and imagination. I want to express my grateful thanks to: an extraordinary editor, Joseph Montebello; a supportive and insightful agent, Al Zuckerman; Norman Currie of Bettman Archives, whose dedication to finding the perfect image never flagged; Howard Mandelbaum of Photofest, who seemed to have as much fun as I did searching through the "golden age" of Hollywood for the perfect shot; Deborah and Peter Hughes, whose computer skills revised a disorganized mountain of disks; Stephen Houy-Towner and Deirdre Donohue of the Irene Lewisohn Costume Reference Library of the Metropolitan Museum of Art and the reference staff of the Fashion Institute of Technology (F.I.T.) library, whose help enabled me to compile a comprehensive history of accessories.

INTRODUCTION

If you open the top drawer of a woman's dresser, chances are you will find: five scarves in assorted sizes, a white linen gardenia pin, turquoise earrings bought on vacation in Arizona, and a Bakelite bracelet discovered in a flea market. What do these items have in common? They've never been worn.

Accessories are appealing. They look wonderful in magazines, irresistible in store windows, and seductive in glass showcases. But once in your home, they tend to stay quietly in your dresser. The luminous scarf that promised to go so well with your new lavender suit now seems lumpy and awkward around your shoulders. The white flower never looks quite right with your navy jacket. It almost seems like accessories should come with a set of instructions. Now they do.

Terms of Adornment deals with the shoes, gloves, bags, and jewelry that delight and confound us. From ascots to watches this book looks at the history of each item, examines the different types, and offers fresh ways to wear what you already own, while also serving as a guide to choosing new accessories with confidence. *Terms of Adornment* will empower you, showing how to wear what you like, rather than dictating what is right and wrong. You will find that you are spending less money on clothes, yet look and feel fantastic.

Building a Wardrobe of Accessories

Accessories are often accumulated differently than the rest of the wardrobe. Women rarely set out to buy a specific piece such as a fedora hat or an ivory bracelet. Many pieces are inherited from relatives while others are received as gifts, or are impulse buys on a vacation. A few items are bought to go with specific outfits. This random acquisition can create drawerfuls of lovely but seemingly unrelated pieces. To choose and use the right accessories, it is helpful to divide them into two broad groups: the stars and the supporting players.

Accessory stars such as a faux fur handbag or a pair of oversized rhinestone earrings will always take center stage. The focus of every eye, they are the first thing people will see and the last thing they forget. By virtue of their size, shape, color, or texture, accessory stars make a memorable impact. Your clothing becomes the background canvas for these accessories with attitude.

Subtle, but never boring, supporting players provide balance and finish. Sometimes they reinforce a star, such as a pair of small silver hoop earrings to balance an oversized silver and ivory bracelet. In other situations, supporting accessories are all that's needed with a spectacularly cut or boldly patterned fabric. A good example: a pair of small diamond stud earrings with a sheer black lace slip dress.

Creating a Look

The true goal of this book is to help women wear accessories with confidence. The how-to-wear lists were established on three basic rules: (1) the clothes are flattering to a range of ages and body types; (2) they are contemporary and timeless; and (3) they are widely available at a range of prices.

The basic pants, sweaters, shirts, jackets, dresses, and coats are used repeatedly, recognizing that few of us have unlimited wardrobe budgets. The often-used clothing pieces form the backbone of a basic wardrobe. This certainly doesn't mean that these should be the only items in your closet. We all enjoy finding and wearing new and different styles for diversity and attitude. Just keep in mind that some clothing is too strong to take decoration, while the basics will give you a canvas to use almost any accessory.

The outfits range from trendy to classic, casual to formal, wearable in summer or winter. There are colorful and complex ensembles for the times that you want to be the center of attention as well as monochromatic styles when you want to project a quiet confidence.

Jewelry is used in two distinct ways throughout the book. Small gold or silver hoop earrings and chains, and pearl stud earrings offer a wonderful touch of light and finish to an outfit. If you usually don't wear jewelry this is a good way to develop a comfort level with these always flattering accessories. In other outfits, dramatic pieces such as cuff bracelets or a string of large amber beads add color and focus.

Terms of Adornment is a book to read and enjoy. If you have a favorite accessory, look it up to find new ways to wear it. When there is a piece in your drawers or closet that never seems to get a chance to go out, check out the how-to-wear sections for inspiration. On a rainy afternoon, or lying on a sunny beach, thumb through the pages to find out how to wear a large pin or find the most flattering hat. Write in the book, noting which outfits worked and additions of your own imagination. Add new outfits that you create as well as a wish list of accessories that you'd love to add to your collection. Remember, the only style that matters is your own personal style.

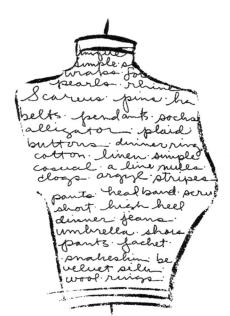

t TERMS OF ADORNMENT

a

ALLIGATOR

In the 1930s and '40s, shoes and handbags of alligator were considered the height of luxury. Paired with elegant brown suede gauntlet gloves, they completed the uniform of the chic and moneyed. Hollywood movie stars carried slim envelope bags or travel satchels as a mark of success, and mass market manufacturers scrambled to copy each accessory.

Alligator is a protected species in many states and therefore genuine skins are expensive. Their characteristic box-like markings are often incised on smooth calf leather to simulate the real thing. Usually seen in brown and black, the textured leather adds depth and shine to shoes, belts, and bags. The effect: a quick hit of luxury that enlivens tailored clothing.

Search vintage clothing stores and established flea markets for the genuine article. With unmistakable retro details—unusual closures, quirky handles—these items were usually designed in strong, simple, surprisingly modern shapes.

How to Wear Alligator

❋ **black alligator loafers**
❋ **black alligator satchel bag**
    black or gray hair bow or clip, or velvet headband
    red cashmere sweater set
    gray flannel trousers
    black suede belt
    red argyle socks
    small marcasite and onyx earrings
    strand of pearls

❋ **black alligator loafers**
    black cashmere crew-neck or turtle neck
    gray flannel trousers
    black-and-white print socks
    small baby gold hoop earrings

❋ **brown alligator loafers**
    tortoiseshell hair clip
    cream wool turtleneck
    cream wool trousers
    brown suede belt
    cream ribbed socks
    amber stud earrings
    brown and navy or pastel printed Hermès-style scarf tied as a man's tie
    gold link bracelet
    brown leather shoulder bag

✿ **brown alligator high-heeled pumps**
✿ **brown vintage alligator clutch**
   brown velvet headband or hair bow
   navy gabardine 1950s-style suit with
     short skirt
   cream notched-collar silk blouse
   brown sheer stockings with back seam
   pearl stud earrings
   gold wristwatch

✿ **brown alligator belt**
   camel crew-neck sweater
   brown and blue Harris tweed blazer
   blue jeans
   brown suede lug-soled loafers
   small thin gold hoop earrings
   blue, green, and cream chiffon scarf

✿ **brown alligator belt**
   white T-shirt
   navy blazer
   blue jeans
   navy-and-cranberry socks
   brown loafers
   gold and pearl earrings

✿ **brown alligator flats**
   tortoiseshell barrette
   short brown linen tank dress
   amber bead necklace

ALPINE HAT

This sporty hat made of felt or tweed has a narrow upturned brim and a soft crown divided by a lengthwise crease. The hat is banded with one or two narrow pieces of muted-color cording or narrow ribbon and is traditionally trimmed with a brush and other mementos. The Tyrolean hat originally served as the lining for Austrian and German soldiers' war helmets. Upon returning home, the soldiers removed the linings and wore them alone, shaping the fabric for a perfect, individualized fit.

The alpine hat is authentic and folkloric, like western cowboy wear, yet sophisticated because it implies that the wearer has traveled. It became popular during the 1930s and '40s, a time that many consider the golden age of men's fashions. It's a hat that can reflect the personality and experiences of the wearer because you can decorate it with your choice of brush, feather, or metal badges from the mountains you've climbed or slopes you've skied. Because of its "plumage" that tends to move, it gives a jaunty casual air much like a tasseled loafer. Worn at a slant, the alpine hat balances bulky winter clothing and adds a touch of originality to tweeds, wools, and shearling.

➤ **TIP: DON'T LOOK LIKE HEIDI**

The charming flavor of the Alpine hat is best worn as an accent to a winter wardrobe. Avoid the temptation to pair it with other Tyrolean items like loden coats and reindeer-patterned scarves. Use a touch of the Tyrol to add style rather than to re-create a regional costume.

How to Wear an Alpine Hat

❂ **taupe felt alpine hat**
cranberry twin sweater set
gray wool mid-calf-length
    pleated skirt
brown leather riding boots
brown shearling-lined suede coat
bone cashmere gloves

❂ **black felt alpine hat with loden band**
black or gray wool pants
black suede lug-soled loafers
red cashmere scarf
black and cream tweed men's overcoat
red wool gloves

❂ **olive wool alpine hat**
red turtleneck
olive wide-wale corduroy jeans
brown riding boots
camel hair duffel coat
tartan gloves

❂ **brown felt alpine hat**
cream cashmere sweater
brown Harris tweed hacking jacket
gray flannel pants
blue and cream argyle socks
brown suede lug-soled loafers
burgundy and green paisley scarf tied
    in a knot

❂ **black alpine hat with olive band**
black turtleneck
Black Watch—plaid wool tartan pants
bottle-green socks
black suede flats
small gold hoops
black wool swing coat
Black Watch—plaid gloves

❂ **loden green alpine hat**
gray long-sleeved knit collar sweater
brown wool pleated trousers
gray patterned trouser socks
brown high-heeled oxfords
pearl earrings
gold Bakelite dog pin at neck
brown and gray tweed coat
loden green gloves

AMBER

Amber comes with centuries of back story. One of the oldest known ornamentations, men and women from the time of the Stone Age wore amber charms to protect them from evil spirits. Warm to the touch and magnetic when rubbed, amber seemed to be drenched with magical powers. Roman soldiers wore amber amulets into battle, Renaissance women clutched strings of amber beads for protection against sorcerers, and Victorian mothers pinned amber charms to their infants' clothing.

Although worn as a gemstone, amber is actually fossilized tree sap. There are basically two types of amber, translucent and opaque. Both kinds can be found in colors ranging from pale champagne to deep brown. Tastes and values vary from region to region. The French treasure the clear and flawless forms while Eastern Europeans prefer cloudy pieces with swirls and tiny fossils.

Jewelry from amber is found in rough, irregularly shaped chunks or polished discs and beads. From the turn of the century to the 1930s, an amber bead necklace was considered an essential item in a woman's wardrobe. If you find amber jewelry in an antique store or are lucky enough to inherit a piece, the amber will have developed a glowing patina. The deep, rich tones reflect on your skin, warming even the palest of winter skins.

Modern pieces are frequently set in silver and look wonderful mixed with other pieces of silver. For example, if you clip on a pair of amber and silver earrings, balance and complement them with a silver cuff bracelet. When you wear more than one piece of amber, choose pieces of similar form and color. Golden tones of amber look best with clothing in tones of brown, green, and burnt orange, and combine beautifully with tortoiseshell, leopard print accessories, and earth-toned shades of Bakelite. Cranberry amber, usually seen in necklaces of faceted beads, brightens navy and gray clothing and is spectacular worn alone with summer whites.

How to Wear Amber

❂ **amber earrings**
❂ **honey-gold amber cuff bracelet**
  taupe gabardine jacket
  black pants
  black suede loafers
  mini-leopard-print scarf around neck
  black Bugatti bag

❂ **double strand of small, chunky amber beads**
  brown linen tank dress
  brown alligator sandals
  ivory earrings
  straw tote bag

❂ **honey-gold amber bead necklace**
bone silk shirt with sleeves rolled up
brown mid-calf suede skirt with side slit
brown sandals

❂ **honey-brown amber and silver earrings**
brown sweater set
gray flannel pants
brown suede loafers
silver cuff bracelet

❂ **necklace of small, clear, brown amber beads**
❂ **amber bracelets**
brown ribbed merino wool turtleneck
    and cardigan sweaters
black pants
brown suede pull-on boots
small gold hoop earrings

❂ **pale, cloudy gold amber earrings**
gray cashmere long-sleeved
    polo sweater

gray flannel pants
brown suede loafers
yellow, gold, and gray ascot
brown woven leather handbag

AMETHYSTS

This February birthstone is often called the queen of quartz. In shades that range from pale lavender to deep purple, amethysts are flattering on virtually everyone. Available in both smooth beads as well as faceted jewels, they look beautiful with silver as well as combined with pearls and gold. In the 1970s purple was the color associated with spirituality and was worn in everything from tiny stud earrings to mid-calf wool coats. Amethysts are particularly versatile, capable of adding warmth to a gray gabardine pantsuit, or a delicate touch of color to a flowered summer dress, and

THE AMBER ROOM

The most extraordinary amber creation is not a piece of jewelry, but an entire room. In 1701, a grand chamber made of twelve intricately carved panels was created for the Prussian King Frederick I. A few years later it was presented to Peter the Great and installed in the Summer Palace near Saint Petersburg. Two centuries later the Nazis removed the panels to "protect" them from Allied bombing. Valued at more than $150 million in 1941, they have never been seen again. Many believe that they are hidden somewhere in Germany, a priceless treasure waiting to be found.

is an unexpected vibrant companion to basic brown.

➤ **TIP**
Don't wear amethysts to the beach, because they fade in strong sunlight.

How to Wear Amethysts

❁ **18-inch strand of amethyst beads** and two silver chains and pendants
lavender silk shirt
gray flannel pants
black suede loafers
small marcasite earrings
silver cuff bracelet

❁ **amethyst and silver earrings**
gray gabardine pantsuit
black high-heeled loafers
silver cuff bracelet
black suede bag

❁ **amethyst and pearl earrings**
black velvet shift
black panty hose
black spike heels
pearl necklace
purple chiffon and cut-velvet stole

❁ **amethyst heart-shaped drop earrings**
beige mid-calf-length linen tank dress
bone linen espadrilles
bone crocheted mini-bag

ANKLE-STRAP SHOES

Ankle-strap shoes were a staple for Hollywood screen sirens of the 1940s. These shoes are meant to be flirtatious rather than simply beautifying, drawing attention to the ankles, a quietly erogenous zone. Keep in mind that the strap tends to shorten the leg, so higher heels might be necessary. Ankle-strap shoes are a natural with basic summer dresses, but they can also be provocative with a linen pantsuit, or with dark lace knee-high socks peeking out from the cuffs of a dark pantsuit.

How to Wear Ankle-Strap Shoes

❁ **navy suede ankle-strap wedge-heeled shoes**
white linen or pique vest blouse
navy-and-white polka-dot pants
white lace-edged ankle socks
red Bakelite bracelet

❁ **light blue open-toed ankle-strap shoes**
light blue and white vintage slip worn as a dress
pale pink vintage beaded sweater
small pearl stud earrings
clear carved Lucite handbag

❂ **black suede ankle-strap
wedge-heeled shoes**
natural straw cloche with black trim
around the crown

cranberry long-sleeved skinny T-shirt
black mid-calf Lycra skirt
black opaque panty hose
jet earrings

AQUAMARINES

There are few stones as flattering to the face as the clear, pale blue aquamarine. The birthstone of March, it has been the universal symbol of youth and hope since the 16th century. Worn as earrings, their sparkle and unique coloring enhance virtually every eye color. Aquamarine looks sensational with pale colors and classic clothing. Worn alone or combined with diamonds or pearls, aquamarine is a special choice with spring and summer clothing. Aquamarine should not be restricted to the soft, pale colors of summer—it lifts muted gray and brown wools, as well as winter whites.

How to Wear Aquamarines

❁ **aquamarine earrings**
  bone cashmere crew-neck
  bone gabardine pants
  cream suede high-heeled loafers
  off-white oblong piece of antique lace
    worn as a scarf

❁ **aquamarine and pearl ring**
  bone linen tank dress
  bone and black Chanel-style slingback
    pumps
  pearl stud earrings
  aquamarine and bone chiffon or
    silk ascot

❁ **pearl and aquamarine ring**
  pale green and white boucle skirt suit
  bone Chanel-style slingback shoes
  pearl earrings
  thin bone envelope bag on
    shoulder bag

❁ **aquamarine heart-shaped drop earrings**
  pale mid-calf flowered dress
  bone ballet flats
  thin 16-inch gold neck chain

ARGYLE

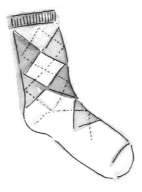

The Duke of Windsor put Scotland on the fashion map when he wore argyle-patterned sweaters and socks while playing his beloved game of golf. A knit interpretation of the traditional tartan plaid of the Argyle clan, it has become a standard accent of fall clothes. If you favor sporty accessories, look for argyle socks in the men's department to find a great finish for cold weather trousers. If you wear trendier clothing, look for a red, white, and black argyle cap and mittens to update last year's black coat. Mixing argyle with other patterns in a fall outfit is a trick of the adventurous. The secret to a successful combination is to choose patterns with similar tones and levels of brightness.

How to Wear Argyle

✿ **brown, yellow, and navy argyle cardigan**
  bone crew-neck
  brown tweed pants
  navy loafers
  navy nylon backpack trimmed with
    brown suede

✿ **red and black argyle wool turtleneck**
  black-and-white-checked long
    wool skirt
  red chunky socks
  black suede lug-soled loafers
  black vintage men's polo coat
✿ **red and white argyle mittens**
✿ **brown, rust, and yellow argyle muffler**
  yellow beret
  brown and white vintage men's coat
  rust gloves

✿ **black and gray argyle socks**
  white linen shirt
  black V-necked cardigan sweater

  gray pants
  black patent leather loafers
  black and silver marcasite
    brooch at neck
  silver cuff bracelet

ASCOT

Originally a standard item in a 19th-century gentleman's wardrobe, this short wide scarf was wrapped around the neck and looped under the chin. As time passed the ascot was used for a touch of informal elegance. Tucked into an open shirt or silk robe, it became the emblem of cosmopolitan style (think Fred Astaire). Chanel popularized the ascot when she wore it to the hounds with Winston Churchill. Gradually women adopted riding habits and all but took over the ascot, using it to add color and panache to tailored blouses and collarless sweaters.

True ascots are designed with a narrow neckband between leaf-shaped pieces of fabric. However, any large silk or chiffon square can be folded into an ascot-friendly shape. Lay the scarf flat and fold corner to corner until it is 6 inches wide. This long thin shape can be wrapped, looped like an ascot around the neck, and tucked into an open-necked blouse.

How to Wear an Ascot

✿ **cranberry paisley ascot**
   camel cashmere crew-neck sweater
   brown or camel pants
   brown-tone print socks
   brown suede loafers
   gold earrings
   gold chain-link bracelets
   brown Bugatti bag

✿ **green print ascot**
   blue men's-tailored shirt
   green cashmere V-necked sweater
   blue jeans
   navy print socks
   blue suede loafers
   pearl stud earrings
   gold link bracelets

✿ **navy polka-dot ascot**
   bone silk notch-collared shirt
   navy oversized V-necked cardigan
   blue jeans
   navy print socks
   red suede loafers
   navy bag

AVIATOR GLASSES

Made famous by General Douglas MacArthur, these wire-rimmed sunglasses were designed to reduce glare from high altitudes for pilots. The rounded ear-piece hooks over the ear to stop the glasses from slipping off when the plane is in a dive or turns sharply in an evasive maneuver. Obviously this is not an issue for most sunglasses wearers, but the rounded ear piece can be an asset when jogging or driving. The sparse, severe lines have a classic elegance that project an air of authority.

b

BACKPACK
(AKA KNAPSACK)

Rugged soldiers' mess packs are the forerunner of the ubiquitous backpack. The word knapsack comes from the Dutch *knappen* ("to eat") and zac ("bag"). The double straps are designed to distribute the load to both shoulders in order to carry as much weight as possible. In nylon and canvas, backpacks are casual hard workers, while in leather or the new black nylon they are more urban and youthful, yet elegant when slung over one shoulder. Choose backpacks with your height in mind. If you are over 5'6", look for packs that are at least 10 inches in length. If you are shorter than 5'4", avoid the oversized packs (more than 15 inches in length)—they will cover your entire back and make you look like a turtle.

How to Wear a Backpack

❁ **small black velvet or nylon backpack**
   black mid-calf wool jumper
   white T-shirt
   black opaque tights
   black Chanel flats
   double strand of chunky pearls
   around the neck or wrist
   pearl stud earrings

❁ **large black leather backpack**
   pink cashmere sweater
   black pleated pants
   black suede boots
   black-and-white men's vintage coat
   black leather gloves

❁ **medium-brown leather backpack**
   black and brown leather riding boots
   camel steamer coat
   small gold hoop earrings

❁ **medium-brown leather backpack**
   white T-shirt
   navy wool blazer
   blue jeans
   navy and brown argyle socks
   brown lizard loafers
   small gold hoop earrings

❁ **black nylon backpack**
   white fine-gauge wool sweater
   black zippered wool jacket
   black wool pants
   black alligator-patterned loafers
   small silver hoop earrings

BAG

black tote of the 1990s. The widening roles of women led to diversified styles for different circumstances—a canvas or straw bag for summer, a leather satchel for work, a fanny pack for running, or a small satin envelope for evening. In the 20th century, the bag is arguably the most significant accessory in the closet.

(Also see BUGATTI BAG, CHANEL BAG, DUFFEL BAG, ENVELOPE BAG, KELLY BAG, MINAUDIÈRE, SATCHEL BAG, SHOULDER BAG, and TOTE BAG.)

BAKELITE JEWELRY

For most of history, woman did not carry bags; they didn't need to. Their dresses were full enough that pockets sewn into the seams could carry all that they needed. After both the French and American revolutions at the end of the 18th century, the antiroyalist fervor introduced a new simplicity in fashion. Instead of full skirts in heavy fabrics, women wore slim gowns of the lightest muslin. There was no way to fashion an invisible pocket in the sheer material, and woman began to carry small drawstring bags hung from their wrists. Even when full hoopskirts came back into fashion, woman continued to carry separate bags. As women became more independent, their lives expanded and so did their bags. Just compare the tiny drawstring bags of the 1800s with the big

Leo Bakeland was a chemist looking for a new material to use for insulation. In the early 1900s he developed a versatile resin that was too attractive to remain hidden in a radio case. Called Bakelite, the plasticlike substance glowed with deep resonant colors that were to inspire jewelry designers for decades. Used for earrings, pins, buckles, buttons, and bracelets, it was the perfect accessory for its time. The colorful, joyous pieces mirrored the culture of the United States between World War I and the Great Depression. In the 1920s, Bakelite jewelry was geometric, inspired by the lines of art deco. By the mid–1930s, styles began to change from angular and modern to carved floral and figural themes. One of the earliest and most popular motifs was the Scottie dog, inspired by President Franklin Roosevelt's favorite dog Fala. Other styles followed including horses, cherries (inspired by Carmen Miranda), palm trees, anchors, and hearts.

Worn with bright print rayon dresses and a jaunty felt hat, they embodied the optimism and sweet innocence of the 1920s. In fact, by 1936, 70% of all costume jewelry sold was made of Bakelite. Less than a decade later in 1945, Bakelite production came to an abrupt halt after the raw materials were requisitioned for war industries. Despite a limited run, Bakelite was so popular that there is quite a bit of Bakelite still around. Many of the pieces are in tones of olive green, gold and tan, and a deep rusty red—perfect if you wear earth tones. Less frequently, you will find pieces in black and bright red or yellow, which pair well with black, white, and primary colors. Polka dots on Bakelite are a rare find—and expensive—but if you do succumb, you'll wear those pieces forever.

How to Wear Bakelite

✿ **large Bakelite horse head pin**
   black beret
   brown and black cowboy boots
   camel coat
   black wool gloves
   brown leather backpack

✿ **brown Bakelite Scottie pin**
   bone cashmere polo sweater
   gray flannel pants
   brown suede loafers
   brown argyle socks
   gold earrings

✿ **red chunky Bakelite bracelet**
   black mid-calf linen shift
   white T-shirt
   black suede wedge shoes

✿ **red Bakelite geometric necklace**
   white long-sleeved shirt
   black skinny pants
   red-and-black polka-dot thin socks
   black Chanel-style flats
   black tank wristwatch
   diamond stud earring

✿ **red Bakelite cherry pin**
✿ **red and white Bakelite bracelets**
   navy pantsuit
   white T-shirt
   black or navy suede loafers
   navy leather bag
   diamond stud earring

❀ **black rhinestone-studded
  Bakelite bangle bracelet**
  black linen shift
  black suede mules
  diamond stud earrings

❀ **gold Bakelite button earrings**
❀ **black and brown Bakelite
  bangle bracelets**
  brown skirt suit with high
    mandarin collar
  black opaque panty hose
  black high-heeled loafers
  black peacoat
  brown muffler
  brown kid leather gloves
  black satchel or tote bag

❀ **earth-tone wide carved Bakelite
  bangle bracelet**
  bone cashmere crew-neck
  olive green corduroy overalls
  Fair Isle socks
  brown suede clogs

❀ **red cherry Bakelite pin on lapel**
  navy-and-white-striped long-sleeved
    T-shirt
  navy linen blazer
  white cotton pants
  navy espadrilles

BALLET FLATS

In mood, ballet flats are dressy; in practice, they're sensible. Styled after ballet slippers, these feminine, comfortable, and charming shoes generate an aura of fragile innocence. It is almost impossi-

THE RIGHT SHOE FOR A NEW LOOK

Street-wear ballet shoes were the inspiration of the innovative American designer Claire McCardell during the wartime shortages of the late 1940s. McCardell was already well into creating the look of American sportswear and needed footwear to complement her collection. She loathed the heavy, awkward wedge and platform shoes of the war years and wanted a lighter, more casual shoe to accessorize her comfortable clothing. McCardell asked Capezio to produce a street-wear version of its ballet slippers with small flat heels and harder soles.

ble not to look graceful when you wear them with a range of skirt lengths.

Ballet flats are inarguably chic when worn with decidedly sporty or tailored clothing. The at-home entertaining uniform of the 1950s socialite often consisted of capri pants in bright silk or satin with a soft sporty sweater and embroidered ballet flats.

Ballet flats are available in a rainbow of colors: basics like black and navy work well with practically everything you own; white and brights such as red, kelly green, and pink add a great shot of color.

Buy these shoes slightly snug since they tend to stretch out. These are not sturdy shoes. Be prepared to replace them frequently if you wear them regularly.

How to Wear Ballet Flats

✿ **black ballet flats**
  white oversized roll-neck pullover
  black skinny pants
  diamond stud earrings

✿ **leopard-print ballet flats**
  black mid-calf linen shift
  pearl stud earrings
  black straw tote bag

✿ **bone ballet flats**
  flowered mid-calf-length slip dress
  straw tote bag

✿ **black ballet flats**
  white cropped polo shirt
  black-and-white-checkered pants
  small gold hoop earrings

✿ **navy ballet flats**
  white sleeveless linen blouse or vest
  mid-calf navy-and-white polka-dot
    skirt
  pearl and gold earrings
  pearl necklace

✿ **red ballet flats**
  navy-and-white-striped cotton
    T-shirt
  white skinny pants
  gold hoop earrings
  red print cotton tote or satchel bag

✿ **black Chanel-style ballet flats**
  black tunic-length wool turtleneck
  flowered mid-calf flannel skirt
  black opaque tights
  pearl stud earrings

✿ **black suede ballet flats**
  black-and-white polka-dot shirt
  black linen shorts
  pearl stud earrings

✿ **red ballet flats**
  white T-shirt
  red cardigan tied around shoulders
  black pants
  small gold hoop earrings
  quilted red print satchel bag

BANDANNA

This print scarf—usually in red or blue and white—was popular with American cowboys of the 1800s. They were used to mop a sweaty brow during cattle drives, or were pulled over the nose and chin when caught in a dust storm. The ban-

danna has come a long way since *Easy Rider* and the urban cowboys of the 1970s who tied bandannas around the legs of their skin-tight jeans. An emblem of cool contemporary style, they are worn with equal confidence by sweat-drenched line dancers, hyperactive rappers, and cheerful preppies.

How to Wear a Bandanna

✿ **red bandanna** to tie up ponytail
white eyelet shirt
white pants
white espadrilles

✿ **blue-and-white bandanna** tied
  backwards on the head
blue skinny T-shirt
white overalls
white sneakers
silver hoop earrings

✿ **red-and-white bandanna**
  knotted around neck and
  tucked in collar
white T-shirt
navy blazer
blue jeans
navy suede loafers
small pearl stud earrings

BANGLE BRACELET

Round, rolling, and often noisy, bangle bracelets were originally called bangle rings because they looked like oversized wedding bands. Bangles range from thin, delicate gold circles to wide, colorful, chunky Bakelite rounds. A single bangle tends to look rather lonely and most devotees wear at least two to three at a time. You can wear a wristful of all gold, all silver, or a mixture of related pieces like ivory and tortoiseshell or a collection of different colors of Bakelite.

When you match bangles to clothing, such as wooden bangles with earth-toned fabrics, the bracelets play a finishing role. If you wear a wide clattering group of bangles or choose high-contrast or eclectic pieces such as colored Lucite, the bracelets become a dominant focus in the look.

How to Wear a Bangle Bracelet

✪ **ivory bangle bracelet**
off-white short-sleeved linen top
peach linen pants
bone linen slides
tiny silver hoop earrings
bone crocheted shoulder bag

✪ **three tortoiseshell bangle bracelets**
cranberry mid-calf linen shift
brown leather platform slides
straw tote bag

✪ **three thin gold bangle bracelets**
(one on the left wrist with a wristwatch, and the other two on the
right wrist)
blue-and-white-striped cotton shirt
khaki shorts
tan driving shoes
cognac small leather Bugatti bag
small gold hoop earrings

✪ **red carved Bakelite bangle bracelet**
navy linen shift
navy ballet flats
gold "baby" hoop earrings
straw tote bag with red cherry corsage

✪ **five thin silver ethnic bangle bracelets**
black short-sleeved turtleneck sweater
black pin-striped pants
black ankle-boots
silver earrings
black nylon tote bag

BARRETTE

Throughout the 19th century, hair for the fashionable woman was an almost architectural arrangement of curls, rolls, and braids. Each style had its own distinct personality and name. Frequently a hair ornament was designed for a specific style. In the late 1870s the hairstyle of the moment was the cadogen, which featured a roll of hair at the base of the neck. To secure the roll, stylists developed what they called *une barrette* or "little bar." The cadogen, along with gas lamps and buggy whips, have disappeared, but the barrette has re-mained an endearing hair ornament.

Big or small, sporty or dressy, they add a youthful exuberance to any look. Barrettes can disguise a bad-hair day, add humor to a quiet outfit or polish to a tailored look. Short hair can look wonderful with small barrettes while long hair is balanced by larger styles.

How to Wear a Barrette

❂ **ivory barrette**
  olive green linen shift
  taupe woven slides
  natural straw tote bag

❂ **tortoiseshell barrette**
  Fair Isle cardigan
  white cotton turtleneck sweater
  camel corduroy pants
  bone cashmere socks
  alligator loafers

❂ **black carved barrette**
  white silk turtleneck
  black silk Chinese jacket
  black mid-calf wool skirt
  black tights
  black Chinese-style flats
  pearl stud earrings

❂ **pearl-trimmed barrette**
  black linen shift
  black ballet flats
  black straw tote bag

❂ **Mickey Mouse barrette**
  white T-shirt
  blue denim overalls
  red high-top sneakers
  pearl wide cuff bracelet

BASEBALL CAP

Baseball caps are one of the few truly American hats. They became popular in the 1920s, part of the mythology that grew up around the sport. Fans wore team hats to express their support as players were exalted to national hero status. For a country deep in the throes of the Great Depression, the cap was cheap, totemic, and distinctly American—the symbol of hope and endurance. Champions such as Babe Ruth made baseball the national sport and the baseball cap the headgear of the nation.

It became the hat of the working man, worn by gas station attendants, truck drivers, and farm workers. Often embellished with professional or commercial logos, it was inclusive by style and selective by message. The baseball cap found a new generation of wearers among college students as they plunged into the political and social revolution of the 1960s.

Baseball caps are worn with equal enthusiasm today by jogging presidents, traveling rock divas, tense SWAT teams, and confident Little League pitchers.

cozy). Most caps are made of canvas, but velvet, wool plaid, suede, and leather—either singly or in combination—are popular fabrics. It is easy to collect new favorite styles and colors—the trick is stopping.

How to Wear a Baseball Cap

❀ **navy baseball cap**
white T-shirt
navy blue blazer
blue jeans
red and navy argyle socks
white Keds

❀ **black baseball cap**
black T-shirt with white lettering
black pants
black high-heeled loafers

❀ **white canvas baseball cap**
white T-shirt
white shorts
red driving shoes

❀ **navy baseball cap**
white T-shirt
white pants
white slip-on Keds

❀ **black baseball cap**
white T-shirt
gray sweatpants
white sneakers

No longer a bold fashion statement, baseball caps have become a part of the fashion landscape. On women they provide a look of boyish, enthusiastic machismo, a sense of being part of a team—in contrast to the rugged individualism of the cowboy hat.

The long visor flatters most noses, while the adjustable back guarantees a custom fit. We wear them for active sports, on bad-hair days, and even to keep warm (in wool they are surprisingly

BELT

Like many accessories, belts began as a necessity and ended up as decoration. Worn around or just below the waist, belts can be tied, buckled, or pulled through loops and buckled. Whatever their shape and size, belts define a silhouette. A gray suede belt offers polish, a fabric sash provides softness and movement, while a tooled leather cowboy belt adds texture and a sense of nostalgia. If your belt is the same tone as your top, it will lower the waistline. When it is the same color as your pants or skirt, your waist will appear shorter and your legs longer. If the belt is a different color from the rest of the clothing, it will cut the body in half—fine if you are tall. If you're not, echo the color in your shoes to draw the eye up and near the face—the eye will then travel from top to bottom, creating a longer look. The best belt balances the impact of texture, color, and contrast.

How to Wear a Belt

❀ **black patent leather belt**
 black crew-neck sweater
 black pants
 leopard-print shoes
 silver earrings
 silver cuff bracelet

❀ **tan ½-inch-wide leather belt with white stitching**
 white oversized linen men's-tailored
  shirt, unbuttoned at the neck,
  sleeves rolled to elbows
 white handkerchief-linen
  pleated pants
 thin white socks
 tan leather ballet flats
 strand of pearls
 natural straw tote bag with
  brown leather straps

❀ **Native American bead belt**
 white cotton shirt
 blue jeans
 white crew socks
 navy ballet flats
 silver earrings

❀ **black suede belt with large silver buckle**
 black turtleneck
 black mid-calf wool skirt
 black cowboy boots
 small silver hoop earrings
 silver cuff bracelet

❁ brown alligator belt

tan crew-neck sweater
gray flannel pants
brown alligator loafers
brown paisley socks
gold earrings
gold link bracelet

❁ jeweled belt

white silk T-shirt
black softly pleated silk pants
black ballet flats
diamond stud earrings

❁ black 1-inch-wide patent leather belt

black short linen shift
black and tan slingback pumps
opal earrings
black quilted Chanel-style bag

❁ brown lizard belt

brown mid-calf linen shift
brown suede sandals
amber earrings
amber bracelet

BERET

Girls! It's the Genuine French Beret

35¢ EACH

OR THREE for $1.00

Lowest Price in America for Genuine All Wool *French Berets!*

■ Imported from France

Few pieces of clothing have been adopted by so many varied groups of people living in different periods of history as the beret. Worn as military headgear in ancient Greece, the mark of an artist in 19th-century Europe, and the symbol of a revolutionary on the head of Che Guevara, and almost synonymous with French national style, the basic beret varies little. This circular flat shape of wool felt can be sporty when worn close to the head facing forward or jaunty when tipped to the side; when pulled down to cover all or part of the forehead, it is more dramatic. Inexpensive and hardy, berets are available in a range of colors.

H o w   t o   W e a r   a   B e r e t

❁ **cranberry beret**
   off-white turtleneck sweater
   brown corduroy pants
   cranberry-and-gray-speckled socks
   brown hiking boots
   brown quilted jacket
   brown-and-cranberry-striped
     muffler
   cranberry gloves

❁ **camel beret** with Bakelite pin
   off-white crew-neck sweater
   gray flannel pants
   brown paisley socks
   brown ankle-boots
   gold earrings
   gold chain bracelets
   tan polo coat

❁ **black beret**
   black mid-calf skirt
   pale pink turtleneck
   black cowboy boots
   pearl stud earrings
   black and white vintage men's coat
   black and pink argyle wool gloves

❀ **navy beret**
    yellow turtleneck sweater
    gray flannel pants
    gray ribbed trouser socks
    brown suede loafers
    brown backpack
    navy peacoat
    Black Watch–plaid scarf
    navy leather gloves

❀ **black velvet painter's beret**
  with satin bow
    ruby velvet ankle-length dress
    black velvet mules
    diamond stud earrings
    ruby velvet clutch

BLUCHERS

A boarding school favorite, this casual style of oxford was originally named after Field Marshal von Blücher of Prussia. They are sturdy but softer and lighter than traditional oxfords. If you're past prep school age, bluchers work well with chinos and jeans—great for walks in the country, pushing a stroller, or trooping through museum halls.

THE SECRET TIE

The thin laces of bluchers tend to slip loose. To deal with this nuisance, a creative preppy developed an original knotting system. After he pulled the laces tight, he tied and wrapped them at the last grommet. The trick caught on and became the mark of a knowing insider.

How to Wear Bluchers

❀ **bluchers**
    white polo shirt
    chino pants
    pale yellow crew socks
    gold hoop earrings

❀ **bluchers**
    blue sleeveless denim shirt
    chino shorts
    pearl stud earrings

❀ **bluchers**
    white T-shirt
    Black Watch–plaid flannel shirt
    blue jeans
    16-inch pearl necklace

BOA

Sexy, luxurious, and often over-the-top, this long, fluffy scarf of feathers is certainly not everyday wear. Frequently the accessory of choice for five-year-olds playing dress-up, divas, and stylish cross-dressers, they are also extremely flattering, softening lines and flaws better than a pink gel over a spotlight. Boas are usually made of two types of feathers, marabou and ostrich.

Boas elevate the degree of dressiness. Toss a black boa over a plain black crepe shift and you're ready for a black-tie event. Circle one closely around your neck to make a dinner suit more glamorous. Try wearing a boa in an unexpected way, draping it over a black-and-white pin-striped pantsuit.

How to Wear a Boa

❀ **black boa over one shoulder**
   white silk tunic
   black velvet pants
   black satin spike heels
   diamond stud earrings

❀ **white boa around the neck**
   white long crepe tank dress
   white suede spike slingbacks
   diamond stud earrings

❀ **black boa worn as a shawl**
   black strapless cocktail dress
   black satin spike heels
   black pearl stud earrings

❀ **black boa draped over the neck**
   black velvet suit
   black sheer panty hose
   black satin high-heeled slingbacks
   pearl and diamond earrings

LESS IS MORE

Let the boa be the star. It's very easy to overdo it with a boa, so if you're going for an elegant look, keep the rest of your accessories simple. For example, wear diamond stud earrings rather than long drop earrings, or if you wear long earrings, skip the necklace. Avoid prints, sequins, and patterned hosiery or shoes.

BOATER HAT

Paired with a striped shirt and white flannel pants, the boater was the unofficial 19th-century summer uniform of boating enthusiasts. Originally introduced in the Bedfordshire town of Luton, its popularity spread throughout Europe and the United States. Created from straw that was plaited and coiled into shape, it was too appealing to stay just on a boat. The ribbon-trimmed boater became THE hat for giggling school girls, serious clergymen, and nervous suitors. How the hat was worn became an important issue. Tipped, it implied attitude. Just how tipped and how far forward or to the side was a matter of conscience and courage. In the 1920s, Maurice Chevalier made a straw

boater tipped to a rakish angle a trademark of his cheeky charm. Modern young women wore it flat on the head or set back slightly (think Gigi) for a vigorous game of tennis or ice hockey.

The rather narrow brim and flat crown complement small features, but exaggerate prominent chins and strong noses. A bow or flowers attached to the side or back soften the lines with color.

How to Wear a Boater Hat

❀ **boater hat with black ribbon**
   black T-shirt
   black pants
   black Chanel-style flats
   pearl stud earrings

❀ **boater hat**
   white T-shirt
   black-and-white-print wrap skirt
   black espadrilles
   pearl earrings

❀ **boater hat**
   red-and-white-striped shirt
   white pants
   red suede loafers
   pearl earrings
   white canvas bag

❀ **boater hat**
   white T-shirt
   flowered slip dress
   black and white Chanel-style flats
   pearl earrings

BOOTS

Originally men wore boots for protection while hunting for food and battling for honor. Today women wear boots because they are so damn flattering. Short or tall, plain or fancy, boots add height and slim any silhouette. Boots

lengthen a line by smoothing out the break between the hem of the skirt (or pants) and line of the leg.

The boot section at a well-stocked shoe store is a smorgasbord of possibilities. Red tooled cowboy boots, tan lug-soled hiking or work boots, short brown jodhpur boots, black laced high-heeled granny boots—so many boots, only two feet. Rather than by style, color, or height, boots should be classified by attitude—basic or bold. The former includes black leather riding boots and will be the style you will wear with practically everything except ball gowns and bathing suits. Bold boots are accessory stars—distinctive by cut and material, and ready to add texture and drama.

It is likely that you will wear out a pair of basic boots before they go out of style because of their versatility. However, bold boots are often an impulse buy, a love-at-first-sight purchase, that seem to spend an inordinate time in your closet rather than on your feet. Just because they don't get out much doesn't mean they are a fashion mistake. Recognize them as occasional wear and value them for their rare but spectacular impact.

The only factor that limits a boot is pain. A boot that pinches toes or cuts off circulation is definitely not made for walking. Whatever style you choose, take the time to ensure they are comfortable.

How to Wear Boots

☻ **brown leather knee-high boots**
  brown shearling suede coat
  cranberry print Hermès scarf
  bone cashmere gloves

☻ **black knee-high leather boots**
  black and white vintage men's tweed
    overcoat
  pink angora scarf wrapped around neck
  black cashmere gloves
  black suede bag

☻ **brown ankle-boots**
  heather-tone Fair Isle sweater
  brown corduroy pants
  bone ribbed trouser socks
  small pearl stud earrings

☻ **black ankle-boots**
  gray mid-calf wool winter coat
  paisley shawl over one shoulder
  black suede gloves

☻ **black patent leather over-the-knee
  boots**
  black mohair cropped sweater
  black short skirt
  black wide headband

☻ **black work boots**
  white T-shirt under red-and-black-
    checked flannel shirt
  black knit slim-leg pants
  black belt with silver buckle
  chunky ragg socks

BOW

Bows are unabashedly demure and cheerful—that is their value in an outfit, to quickly soften or romanticize.

Bows are frequently worn as hair ornaments on barrettes or headbands or tied over a ponytail. On other accessories, such as handbags, shoes, and hats, bows provide a flirtatious touch. They are usually found in satin or velvet, but bows can be created from practically any material including metal, tortoiseshell, straw, and wool. Full, puffy bows add curves to angular frames while flat bows add charm without bulk.

How to Wear a Bow

☻ **black bow on ponytail**
  red sweater set
  gray flannel pants
  black suede loafers
  gold button earrings
  chunky gold chain bracelet
  black leather arm-bag

☻ **white chiffon scarf tied into bow**
  around the crown of a straw hat
  flowered slip dress
  white ballet flats
  small pearl drop earrings

✿ **navy flat satin bow**
    under white gardenia pinned to
    collar of white silk shirt
navy skirt suit
white silk shirt
navy sheer panty hose
navy slingback pumps
24-inch pearl necklace
navy envelope bag on chain

✿ **black grosgrain ribbon and bow**
    on straw picture hat
black linen shift
black linen mules
pearl stud earrings
pearl cuff bracelet
straw tote bag

✿ black headband trimmed with a
  small **bow**
  red and black plaid jacket
  black skirt
  black sheer panty hose
  black patent leather pumps
  mabe pearl earrings
  black Kelly bag

✿ **black-and-white gingham bow** over
  low ponytail
  white linen tank dress
  white mules
  red Bakelite earrings
  black straw tote bag trimmed
    with a corsage of cherries

✿ natural straw tote bag trimmed
  with a **brown linen bow**
  olive green linen shift
  brown sandals
  ivory earrings
  ivory bangle bracelet

BRACELET

Women of virtually every culture, from Stone Age cave dwellers to English royalty, have strapped bracelets around their wrists. The styles and popularity of bracelets depend heavily on the prevailing sleeve fashions of the day. Greco-Roman women frequently wore large snakelike bracelets that balanced their sleeveless togas. Centuries later, bracelets were seldom worn with the full, long sleeves of the Middle Ages. With contemporary clothing, there are different sleeve styles and lengths depending on the season and the occasion. Whatever bracelet style you choose, keep in mind how much of the piece will be visible.

Sleeveless, strapless, and short-sleeved blouses focus more attention on a bracelet. A single 2- to 3-inch cuff balances the long expanse of bare arm while a skinny bracelet could be overwhelmed. With long-sleeved jackets, blouses, and sweaters, a large cuff could feel bulky and look clumsy, while several skinny bracelets peeking out from under the sleeve add a flirty flash of gold or silver.

How to Wear a Bracelet

✿ **white chunky pearl bracelet**
  white sleeveless vest
  blue-and-white polka-dot pants
  navy mules
  pearl stud earrings
  straw tote bag

❁ **brown stretchy amber bracelet**
  brown linen shift
  brown alligator-patterned sandals
  amber and silver earrings
  bone linen tote bag

❁ **diamond tennis bracelet**
  combined with pearl bracelet
  black sleeveless shift
  black pumps
  pearl earrings

❁ **silver cuff bracelet**
  black long-sleeved crew-neck sweater
  black pants
  silver "bean" earrings
  black Belgian loafers

❁ **two skinny gold chain bracelets on**
  one wrist
❁ wristwatch and **gold chain bracelet**
  on the other wrist
  bone silk notched-collar shirt
  navy blazer
  blue jeans
  navy loafers
  small gold hoop earrings
  navy Kelly bag

BRETON HAT

A popular style with a brim that rolls up
all around, the Breton hat was adapted
from headgear worn for centuries by
peasants in Normandy. You will find

Breton hats in both felt and straw with
brims that range from 1 to 3 inches.
There is usually a ribbon around the
crown that is sometimes embellished
with a flower or bow. Wear it set back to
frame the face, or settled down low on
the forehead to make your eyes look
enormous. To flatter your features,
make sure that the brim extends past the
tip of your nose.

The shape and proportions of a
Breton hat can be charming to most
women—the trick is finding the correct
brim size. With a bit of experimenting,
this hat will even suit women who normally can't find flattering headgear.

How to Wear a Breton Hat

❁ **straw Breton hat**
  black long linen shift
  black wedge sandals
  silver hoop earrings
  silver cuff bracelet

✿ **straw Breton hat**
   white short-sleeved T-shirt
   pastel flowered slip dress
   white ballet flats
   pearl stud earrings

✿ **black felt Breton hat**
   black boots
   red wool coat with black velvet collar
   black Chanel bag

✿ **hunter green felt Breton hat
with black trim**
   black suede boots
   green wool coat
   black suede envelope bag

✿ **straw Breton hat with black ribbon
and sunflower**
   black short-sleeved cotton shirt
   black linen pants
   black Chanel-style flats
   pearl stud earrings
   pearl necklace
   large black tote bag

BROGUES

Now a walking symbol of conservative elegance, brogues began as a humble Irish working-man's shoe. The holes in the oxford-style shoe were designed to facilitate water drainage while laborers worked in the watery Irish bogs. As time passed the sturdy, beautiful shoes were adopted by the English gentry for shooting and walking in the forests of their country estates. The brogues' position in fashion was secured in 1930s when the Prince of Wales made it one of his favorite casual styles. Designers adapted the brogue for women by adding a higher heel, fringed tongue, or a strap rather than laces across the instep.

Brogues are usually made of smooth leather or suede in black, navy, and shades of brown. Drenched in tradition, they are a wonderful cold weather shoe when worn with tweeds, plaids, and gray flannel. Their sturdy lines demand hearty hosiery such as ribbed tights or argyle socks. Brogues with trendy lugged soles add a hip, ironic look to full pant legs, 1970s-inspired ankle-length skirts, and skinny-leg jeans and khakis.

How to Wear Brogues

✿ **brown-and-cream two-tone brogues**
   peach oblong chiffon scarf tied into
      a 1940s-style hair bow on side of head
   peach, brown, cream, and
      yellow Hawaiian shirt
   brown Shetland sweater
   brown flannel pants
   brown cowboy belt
   brown and peach argyle socks
   brown vintage leather
      "cowboy-look" shoulder bag

❀ **cognac suede brogues**

bone twin set
brown tweed pants
cream cashmere socks
gold "shrimp" earrings
pearl necklace
cranberry-toned paisley shawl

❀ **brown leather brogue tie shoes**

cranberry sweater
brown mid-calf corduroy skirt
cream opaque ribbed tights
garnet and gold earrings
gold chain-link bracelets
brown suede jacket

❀ **cordovan brown brogue loafers**

red twin set
gray flannel pants
paisley socks
small pearl stud earrings
gold link choker
brown suede shoulder bag

❀ **navy brogue loafers**

off-white silk shirt
navy blazer
khaki pants
navy and red argyle socks
small gold hoop earrings
three gold chain-link bracelets

BROOCH

Most of us use the words "brooch" and "pin" interchangeably, but technically speaking, the former was intended to be decorative while the latter was usually functional, holding a garment in place. Common brooch themes include a flower, cross, or animal decorated with stones, pearls, or an etched design. Floral or bow shapes are inherently feminine, stones add sparkle and color, while bird or butterfly styles add movement.

Brooch shapes and motifs go in and out of fashion. In the 1950s most women over the age of ten owned at least one circle pin. More recently it has been the silver squiggle pinned to suit lapels. Look for a piece that is least 2 inches long. It needs be significant in size to create focus and impact. Brooches are worn on either shoulder, but wearing it on your left side is best. The eye naturally travels from the viewer's left to right, and settles there. A brooch on your right side can be distracting.

How to Wear a Brooch

❀ **marcasite lizard brooch** pinned at shoulder
   black crew-neck sweater
   black pants
   black ribbed trouser socks
   black Chanel flats
   diamond stud earrings

❀ **round jeweled brooch** pinned at neck
   white collared shirt
   black jacket
   black pants
   black Chanel flats
   pearl stud earrings
   pearl cuff bracelet

❀ **rhinestone bow brooch** pinned at shoulder
   black cocktail dress
   black panty hose
   black satin pumps
   diamond stud earrings

❀ **gold feather brooch** pinned to black
   felt cloche hat
   black boots
   black vintage men's wool coat

❀ **gold flower brooch** pinned to lapel
   navy skirt suit
   white silk shirt
   navy slingback pumps
   pearl and gold earrings
   pearl necklace
   navy leather bag

❀ **vintage wooden horse-head brooch**
   black and brown riding boots
   camel overcoat
   brown leather backpack

❀ **Bakelite cherry brooch** pinned to overalls strap
   white turtleneck sweater
   denim overalls
   navy ballet flats

❀ **large rhinestone brooch** fastened to bag
   red wool skirt suit
   black sheer panty hose
   black slingback pumps
   black enamel and pearl earrings
   black suede envelope bag

BUCKS

Before the Gucci loafer with the snaffle bit, before the two-tone Chanel pump, the ultimate status shoe was the pale buckskin oxford known as "bucks." In a country struggling to survive the Great Depression, a man who could afford to

uniform at the Ivy League colleges until the 1960s when it was discarded in the cultural revolution that also swallowed the rep tie, white gloves, and the pageboy. This marvelous classic is a natural in summer. Wear it with at least one other piece of preppie style such as khakis, button-downs, or madras, but tweak it a bit for a more updated look. For example, try a pair with a ribbon-trimmed camisole under a button-down Brooks Brothers shirt.

How to Wear Bucks

✿ **tan bucks**
   white polo shirt
   pink cotton crew-neck tied
     around shoulders
   pink plaid pants
   tan and pink argyle socks
   pearl stud earrings
   gold chain bracelet

✿ **tan bucks**
   white T-shirt
   navy blazer
   tan chino pants
   small gold hoop earrings
   gold chain bracelet

✿ **white bucks**
   white T-shirt
   yellow V-necked cardigan
   white pants
   yellow-and-white polka-dot socks

buy shoes just for sport was considered truly wealthy. Born out of the sporting games of America's most privileged in the 1930s, bucks became an instant status symbol. Synonymous with wealth and privilege, white bucks are the reason why so many old-money law firms and brokerage houses became known as "white shoe" companies.

Bucks remained part of the unofficial

❀ **tan bucks**
   white button-down shirt
   Fair Isle sweater
   tan chino pants
   pale blue socks
   pearl stud earrings

❀ **bone suede bucks**
   bone slouchy pantsuit
   white T-shirt
   diamond stud earrings

❀ **white bucks**
   blue-and-white-striped oxford
      shirt over ribbon-edged camisole
   blue jeans
   tooled leather belt
   white crew socks
   small gold hoop earrings

❀ **white bucks**
   white T-shirt
   blue and white seersucker jacket
   khaki pants
   white socks
   14-inch strand of small pearls
   navy-and-white polka-dot floppy
      handkerchief in front pocket

❀ **white bucks**
   white oxford button-down shirt
   navy blazer with gold buttons
   gray flannel pleated pants
   gold-and-navy-striped web belt
   gold and navy argyle socks

BUGATTI BAG

Created by Hermès in 1923 for the Bugatti family, this was the first bag to use a zipper closure. The flat bottom with gently sloping sides was designed to carry sports equipment and clothing in an open sports car. The Bugatti family now manufactures their own version while the Hermès model is called the Bolide bag.

Whether Hermès, Bugatti, or a well-made copy, this bag is roomy but not bulky. The classic, simple lines work well in a range of colors and materials. In textured, conservative leathers, the Bugatti is casually elegant, just about perfect with tailored pants and blazers. In patent leathers, faux furs, or bright colors it adds style and humor to both business and leisure styles.

How to Wear a Bugatti Bag

❀ **caramel pigskin Bugatti bag**
   bone cashmere crew-neck
   brown tweed blazer
   camel gabardine pants
   paisley socks
   brown driving loafers
   small gold hoop earrings

✿ black leather Bugatti bag
white cropped turtleneck
black mid-calf knit skirt
black ankle-boots
silver earrings
silver cuff bracelet

✿ navy leather Bugatti bag
navy pantsuit
white silk shirt
yellow cashmere sweater knotted
   over the shoulders
navy suede loafers
gold knot earrings
gold "San Marco" bracelet

✿ brown-and-black leopard-patterned Bugatti bag
black pantsuit
black turtleneck
black ankle-boots
small but wide silver hoop earrings
silver cuff bracelet

✿ cognac Bugatti bag
cranberry cashmere turtleneck
tweed pants
brown ankle-boots
brown paisley socks
small pearl stud earrings

BUTTONS

Buttons are rather unique accessories because they started out as decorative elements but ended up becoming functional. Greeks and Romans fashioned buttons out of shells, gold, and ivory and attached them on their tunics as decoration. Not until the 14th century, when a particularly creative tailor invented the buttonhole, did buttons become fasteners. Once buttons became popular, there was no stopping them. Tailors seemed driven to find new places to position buttons and buttonholes. Slits were made along sleeves and down legs just to add working buttons. Some women's dresses used as many as 200 buttons to close the back of their gowns.

Designers have enjoyed using buttons for emphasis. Elsa Schiaparelli, the French designer of the 1920s, created a series of colorful Bakelite circus acrobat buttons as fasteners for elegant black jackets and dresses. Patrick Kelly was an

WHY MEN BUTTON FROM LEFT TO RIGHT

One theory is that in the days when men carried swords, having buttons on the right made it easier for a man to unbutton his coat with his left hand, freeing his right hand to draw a sword and defend his honor. Swords as an accessory have disappeared, but the tradition remains.

USING BUTTONS AS ACCESSORIES

- Change the buttons on a black wool peacoat to gold for a dressy look, or use black woven leather for a sporty attitude.
- Sew carved green vintage glass buttons onto a green cashmere cardigan.
- Collect bright children's plastic 1950s buttons from flea markets and use them to line the collar and pocket flaps of a blue or white denim jacket.
- Collect vintage Bakelite buttons with loops on the backs. String elastic through all the loops to make a unique bracelet.
- Change the buttons on a white cashmere cardigan to white round pearl buttons.

- Try brushed gold buttons (often found at flea markets and auctions) on a red, gray, blue, navy, or black cashmere cardigan.
- Add shiny black buttons to a white linen jacket and wear with a black linen shift dress and two-tone black-and-white pumps.
- Change the buttons on a white pique vintage men's tuxedo vest to rhinestones, remove the back and add a white or black satin ribbon to tie it across your bare back. Wear the vest with a pantsuit and diamond earrings.
- Add rounded pearl buttons to a blue-and-green plaid flannel shirt and wear it as a lightweight summer jacket with white cotton beach pants.

American expatriate fashion designer living in Paris in the 1980s; whole collections of his tight, sexy dresses and suits were decorated with all sizes and colors of buttons. When modern designers use unusual buttons to inject humor into their minimalist suit silhouettes, the buttons are often the only "jewelry" needed to accessorize the outfit.

Less expensive clothing is usually produced with plain utilitarian buttons. Changing them to more interesting colors and shapes adds a quick shot of style and taste. Go to your closet and take a fresh look at some of your old basics. Think about replacing ordinary black buttons on a black cardigan with small rhinestone studs, or switching plastic navy buttons to shiny silver squares on a navy blazer. Keep an eye out for old Bakelite or glass buttons to add a touch of vintage originality and focus to your clothing.

c

CAMEO

 Utterly feminine, cameos have a raised design carved into multilayered stones or shells. The white design appears on a pink, brown, or black background. The majority of cameos are made from shells, coral, onyx, and lava stone.

Cameos were first worn in ancient Greece and Rome, and although originals from these periods are usually found only in museums, their classical motifs have remained popular for centuries. You will find pins, earrings, and bracelets with cameos of varying size, design, and color.

The fragile beauty of a cameo is a natural partner for pastel linens, winter white knits, and filmy scarves. Surprisingly they can be equally effective with brown and gray tailored clothing, taking the edge off severe lines and rough textures. Whether you wear them to complete a romantic look, or as a counterpoint to a tweed menswear look, cameos blend beautifully with pearls, diamonds, coral, and gold.

How to Wear a Cameo

✿ **cameo bracelet**
   lime green linen shift
   bone Chanel slingback pumps
   pearl earrings
   delicate gold necklace
   bone pouch shoulder bag

✿ **cameo earrings**
   pale pink mid-calf linen shift
   bone mules
   pearl bracelet
   bone Kelly bag

✿ **cameo pin** on lapel
   gray pantsuit
   gray ribbed trouser socks
   black Belgian loafers
   pearl earrings
   gold bracelet
   black satchel bag

✿ **cameo ring**
   bone crew-neck sweater
   peach, cream, and brown scarf tucked
      into neckline
   brown tweed riding jacket
   tan gabardine trousers
   brown ankle-boots
   small gold hoop earrings
   gold chain bracelets
   brown pigskin Bugatti bag

✿ **cameo pin**
   brown wool pantsuit
   peach cashmere crew-neck sweater
   brown suede ballet flats
   gold and pearl Victorian
      drop earrings
   gold bangle bracelet
   vintage beaded mesh bag

❀ **cameo earrings**
❀ **cameo ring**
  black pantsuit
  white silk shirt
  black Belgian loafers
  gold "San Marco" chain bracelet
  black Kelly bag

CARTWHEEL HAT

This is a hat for women who love to wear hats. Big and round with a low crown and a firm brim, the cartwheel will be the first thing people will see and the last feature they will forget. A full-size cartwheel dominates any room it enters.

There are two schools of thought about the best way to wear this big beautiful hat. Some tilt it back to create an extraordinary frame for the face. Others place it low and flat, a style that creates madly flattering shadows that seems to erase tiny lines and give you great cheekbones.

The large brim is best balanced by some height. If you stand less than 5 feet 5 inches, this hat can make you look shorter. If you stand tall, this hat adds grace, balance, and glamour. The cartwheel is one of those rare accessories that can both chisel off pounds on a large frame and add curves to a thin silhouette.

How to Wear a Cartwheel Hat

✪ **black straw cartwheel hat**
  black short linen shift
  black high-heeled pumps
  pearl earrings
  pearl cuff bracelets

✪ **white straw cartwheel hat** with brown
    ribbon around the crown
  brown-and-white polka-dot dress
  white slingback pumps
  pearl earrings

✪ **off-white cartwheel hat**
  pastel flowered silk dress
  black patent leather slingback pumps
  pearl drop earrings
  black patent leather sling shoulder bag

CHAINS

Chains add an intense hit of light and movement to any look. For centuries chains had been used primarily as a device to hang something, but Chanel popularized chains in their own right. She piled on chains of different weights and lengths to disguise what she felt was an unattractive bustline. It

CHAINS OF CHOICE

There are dozens of styles of chains offered in a range of weights and materials. The five most popular are:

1. ROPE CHAINS: Sturdy and reasonably priced, they are fairly simple to repair.

2. HERRINGBONE CHAINS: The most popular flat chain worn today. It is shinier than most other styles, but tends to tangle and break easily and is very difficult to repair.

3. SOLID LINK CHAINS: These are elegant, strong, and flexible, they hang beautifully and repair with ease. Made with genuine materials, they are more expensive than other chains.

4. BOX CHAINS: Lightweight with a bright reflective surface. They are easy to repair and resist tangling.

5. "SAN MARCO" CHAINS: Also called "fancy chain," the serpentine links are usually seen in medium-weight gold bracelets and short necklaces. A hollow chain, it is designed for business dress rather than active sports.

worked better than she could have ever
imagined. Since that time, women's
drawers have harbored a tangled collection of chains.

In gold or silver (real or faux), different lengths work best for different
silhouettes. For example, a thin 14- to
16-inch gold neck chain, a tiny gleam, is
perfect with a bathing suit or a small
white T-shirt and a pair of jeans. Or, try
one or several 24-inch medium-weight
chains under a notched-collar silk shirt,
or V-neck cardigan.

As a general rule, coordinate chains
in color, style, and weight with the other
pieces you are wearing. A pair of tiny
diamond stud earrings are balanced by a
thin, short chain. Silver earrings the size
of quarters will look just right with a
bracelet or necklace chain of chunky silver links.

How to Wear Chains

❀ **24-inch medium-weight gold
chain-link necklace**
navy pantsuit
off-white notched-collar silk shirt
large red paisley scarf
navy ribbed trouser socks
navy loafers
pearl earrings
navy Bugatti bag

❀ **14- to 16-inch gold rope chain
necklace**
red sweater set
gray flannel pants
gray and red argyle socks
black Belgian loafers
pearl stud earrings
black Kelly bag

❀ **24-inch silver solid link chain
necklace**
white shirt
red pullover tied around the shoulders
black skinny pants
white sneakers
silver hoop earrings
black nylon backpack or tote bag

❀ **two gold chains on one wrist,
one wristwatch and gold chain
on the other**
cream cashmere crew-neck
brown quilted jacket
brown tweed or plaid pants
brown alligator belt
cranberry and brown paisley socks
brown suede loafers
pearl and gold earrings

❀ **"San Marco" chain necklace**
red wool suit
black sheer panty hose
black pumps
mabe pearl earrings
black Chanel or Kelly bag

CHANEL BAG

 A quilted bag on a long chain is synonymous with Coco Chanel's style, but it was actually created late in her career. In 1956, she introduced her first collection after a 17-year self-imposed exile. Accustomed to her minimalist knits of the 1930s, the French didn't know how to react to the bulky pastel knits, laden with thick strands of pearls, quilted bags, and large pieces of costume jewelry, but Americans loved it all. Chanel had designed a bag that was simple in design and elaborate in texture. It was perfect for tailored suits, coats, and dresses, always elegant yet never bland.

The original Chanel bag is one of the most copied styles in fashion history. It is a tribute to the rightness of the original proportions that its charm can survive mass production. This is going to be a bag that you will enjoy for years, so buy one that costs a little more than you would normally spend.

How to Wear a Chanel Bag

❀ **black Chanel bag**
red wool skirt suit
black short-sleeved crew-neck sweater
black sheer panty hose
black pumps
pearl and gold earrings

❀ **black Chanel bag**
black coatdress
black very sheer panty hose
black slingback pumps
coral and pearl earrings
pearl necklace

❀ **bone Chanel bag**
black linen or pique shift
bone and black Chanel-style
  slingback shoes
pearl earrings
coral and pearl
  necklace

❀ **navy Chanel bag**
navy gabardine skirt suit
sheer panty hose
navy slingback pumps
garnet and pearl earrings

❀ **black Chanel bag**
black pantsuit
black-and-white print
  silk blouse
red cashmere sweater tied over
  shoulders
white lace trouser socks
black Chanel-style flats
gold earrings
black and gold
  enamel bracelet

❁ **black Chanel bag**
  black-and-white-plaid jacket
  black miniskirt
  black sheer panty hose
  black patent leather spike heels
  black enamel and pearl earrings
  gold bangle bracelets

❁ **black Chanel bag**
  pink linen jacket
  black short skirt
  black sheer panty hose
  black patent leather pumps
  pearl cluster earrings
  gold bangle bracelets

❁ **black Chanel-style bag**
  green, blue, and black boucle jacket
  black skirt

  black panty hose
  bone and black Chanel-style slingback
    pumps
  mabe pearl earrings
  pearl cuff bracelet

❁ **bone Chanel bag**
  cream gabardine pantsuit
  bone ribbed trouser socks
  black and bone Chanel-style flats
  diamond stud earrings

❁ **small red Chanel bag** worn across
    the chest
  white turtleneck
  blue denim overalls
  red high-top sneakers

INSIDE A REAL CHANEL BAG

The classic quilted bag, known as the 2.55 (its date of birth), was designed to be both functional and beautiful. The exterior, quilted in a diamond-shaped pattern, gives the bag volume and shape. Inside the double flap is a zip-fastened pocket, perfect for hiding secret love letters. The cranberry interior (the color of the uniform in the orphanage where Chanel grew up) is divided into three generous bellows. The color is not just symbolic for Madame Chanel, but designed to provide visibility—an issue that every woman understands when she is trying to find her keys while standing in a darkened hallway. Finally, like an artist's finishing touch, the rectangular clasp and chain are both plated with real gold.

CHANEL SHOES

Arguably the most copied shoe style of the 20th century, the black-toe-capped footwear was part of Coco Chanel's return to fashion in the early 1950s. From the start, it was a shoe hardwired for success, working equally well with pastel winter wools and summer silks and linens. Worn with light-colored hose, the shoe seems to make feet look smaller and legs slimmer as it extends the line of the leg.

You can find this timeless classic in a range of combinations, including navy with a white cap and a black cap with a black suede or patent leather shoe. Comfortable and always elegant, the Chanel style works equally well in flats, pumps, and slingbacks.

How to Wear Chanel Shoes

✿ **black and tan Chanel slingback pumps**
pink short linen dress
black patent leather belt
gold and pearl earrings
black patent leather envelope bag

✿ **navy 2-inch Chanel slingback pumps**
navy coatdress
navy sheer panty hose
garnet earrings
pearl bracelet
small navy shoulder bag

✿ **black Chanel flats**
natural straw boater hat with
    black ribbon
black T-shirt
black linen pants
pearl stud earrings
pearl cuff bracelet
black straw tote bag

✿ **black suede Chanel flats**
black snood with black velvet bow
black cashmere crew-neck sweater
black wool pin-striped pants
white lace socks
diamond stud earrings

CHARMS

The highly personal charm bracelet began in the sentimental Victorian era. Women collected round coinlike "love tokens" from admirers and hung them on large pins or bracelets. In the 1930s the charm bracelet, along with saddle shoes and pastel sweaters, became part of the unofficial uniform of college girls. Instead of love tokens, the charms were

symbolic of the emerging role of women. These bracelets were hung with tiny rulers, date books, cigarette lighters, and champagne bottles.

Charm bracelets became a joyful, jingling collection of personal history, a physical reminder of adventures, interests, beliefs, and dreams. As time passed, the chunky bracelet cluttered with memories became popular with women of all ages. During the social changes of the 1960s, it was banished to the back of the jewelry box as another symbol of the establishment.

Charms are now worn just a few at a time on a long chain, but the symbolism is still there. Look in flea markets and thrift shops for vintage charms that reflect parts of your unique personality. If you have a bracelet of charms, dust it off and wear it to express originality in an era of minimalist style.

H o w t o W e a r C h a r m s

❀ charm bracelet
chartreuse long sweater
black short skirt
black opaque tights
chunky high-heeled loafers
small gold earrings

❀ charm bracelet
black mid-calf linen tank shift
black mules
pearl stud earrings
black straw tote bag

❀ charm bracelet
red sweater set
gray flannel pants
black-and-white polka-dot socks
black patent leather loafers
black Kelly bag

CHOKER

Elegant and often formal, the choker is a necklace worn high on the throat. The classic choker is made of two to five strands of pearls or a strip of black ribbon decorated with a piece of carved coral or a cameo. Both styles soften the lines of a long slender neck, an effect that is at once romantic and regal.

Most women can easily handle a two-strand pearl choker, but wider styles are not as wearer-friendly. This is not a necklace to toss on casually and dash out the door. The neckline should be clear of other distractions such as collars, lapels, and prominent earrings. Because chokers focus attention on your face, hair and makeup should be fresh and polished.

How to Wear a Choker

❁ **double-strand pearl choker**
red collarless jacket
black short skirt
black sheer panty hose
black spike heels
black envelope bag

❁ **black velvet ribbon with small cameo** worn around the neck
white organdy blouse
black cigarette pants
black velvet ballet flats
small pearl stud earrings

❁ **four-strand pearl choker with diamond clasp**
navy off-the-shoulder velvet cocktail dress
pale-toned panty hose
navy silk spike pumps
small silver minaudière

❁ **four-strand pearl choker**
white strapless evening gown
white high-heeled satin sandals
small pearl and diamond earrings

CLOCHE HAT

The cloche (which is French for bell) is a tight little hat, reportedly created by Chanel at the turn of the century when she was still a local milliner in Deauville. The trim shape provided the perfect balance to the slim, narrow silhouette of the 1920s. Usually made of felt, it was an equal-opportunity hat worn by struggling shop girls, elegant debutantes, and serious matrons. It is still a wonderful choice for narrow, tailored coats, particularly if your hair is cropped short. The modern cloche fits more loosely on the head than its Jazz Age ancestor. They are found in straw for warm weather and wool or felt for winter.

How to Wear a Cloche Hat

✿ **natural straw cloche hat** trimmed
 with black ribbon and pink flowers
 pink cropped linen jacket
 black mid-calf linen skirt
 white short socks
 black suede ankle-strap
  platform shoes
 small pearl drop earrings

✿ **black felt cloche hat**
 white silk shirt
 charcoal men's vest
 black jodhpurs
 black ankle-boots
 small pearl stud earrings
 loosely knotted tie

CLOGS

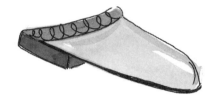

Put on a pair of wood- or cork-soled clogs and you are stepping into the shoes worn by working men for 2,000 years. Simple, sturdy, and inexpensive, clogs were designed to keep the feet warm and

CLOGS AS A POLITICAL STATEMENT

At the start of the Industrial Revolution, workers in France and Belgium protested layoffs by throwing their clogs (called "sabots") into the factory machinery, shutting down production. Their rebellion created a new word—sabotage.

dry. Wood and cork are extremely poor conductors, so body heat does not escape, while the thick soles and heels lift the foot out of water and ice.

Clogs are found in leather, wool, suede, and plastic and in colors that range from plain to fancy. In winter they can be worn with opaque tights and heavy socks. In warmer weather clogs can be worn without hosiery. In any season these chunky charmers are happy to be paired with casual pants and skirts.

How to Wear Clogs

✿ **brown leather clogs**
   white shirt
   blue jeans
   brown leather backpack
   silver link bracelets

✿ **brown suede clogs**
   brown linen dress
   small silver hoop earrings
   ivory and silver cuff bracelet

✿ **black suede clogs**
   cranberry mid-calf long-sleeve dress
   black opaque tights
   cameo earrings

✿ **gray wool clogs**
   white fishermen's sweater
   blue jeans
   small silver hoop earrings
   three silver chain bracelets

✿ **brown leather or suede clogs**
   white cotton shirt
   tan shorts
   small gold hoop earrings
   gold chain bracelets

✿ **black clogs**
   white T-shirt
   black-and-white-print short slip dress
   pearl stud earrings

✿ **yellow rubber clogs**
   white smiley-face T-shirt
   red-and-yellow-plaid pants
   red zippered fanny pack

✿ **tan clogs**
   green mid-calf linen shift
   jade earrings
   straw tote bag

COMB

Decorative hair combs date back to ancient times. Hand-carved from bone and shell, they held back the long hair of wealthy and privileged women. For centuries hair combs were prized and expensive, but after the Industrial Revolution machines were easily able to carve both straight fine teeth and beautiful decorations. Women of more modest means were able to afford combs of tortoiseshell and iron, decorated with filigree and engraving. When Queen Victoria became empress of India in 1876, ivory combs became "the" comb to arrange in towering complicated hairstyles.

Combs are an intensely feminine accessory. Those with delicate narrow teeth work beautifully with fine straight hair. Thicker, curly hair needs combs with broad, more widely spaced teeth. They can be used to both tidy and decorate hair. Wear small plain tortoiseshell combs at the sides to create a soft flattering frame for your face. Try jeweled combs to add sparkle and light. If you have medium to long hair add a decorative vintage comb to a chignon or French twist.

A WARDROBE OF COMBS

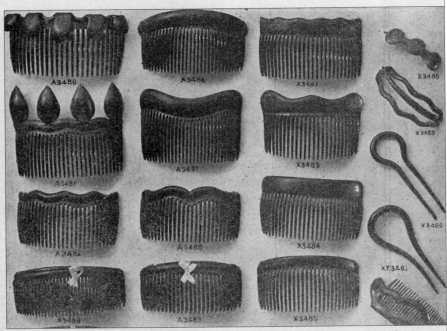

Between 1880 and 1920, hair was arranged to look beautiful from every angle—and combs were used to create this effect. No fashionable woman felt fully equipped without a drawerful of combs in different sizes and materials. There were small combs for the sides, big combs for the back, and special pompadour combs to "garnish" the front. There were even distinctive combs created for specific types of chignons and updo's. Then women began to bob their hair, and almost overnight combs became irrelevant.

CORAL

Looking for an all-purpose accessory? Consider a pair of red coral earrings. They reflect a rosy color on your cheeks, and they were once believed to protect the wearer against sickness and evil.

Coral has been popular in Italy since Roman times. It has remained fashionable there for centuries, perhaps because it is so incredibly flattering to dark hair and eyes. Coral ranges from pale pink (called angel skin) to salmon pink (most common) to deep oxblood red (rather rare). The finest coral is evenly colored, rather than variegated. It is cut into beads, carved into heads, or mounted in cabochon settings. Frequently you will see the natural twigs in coral jewelry, a tradition that began when the Greeks believed that coral's powers were strongest in its natural state.

If you are lucky enough to inherit a piece of coral jewelry, wear it with pearls, gold, and cameos. If you're a coral novice, start of with a pair of coral earrings.

How to Wear Coral

❀ **coral earrings**
❀ **coral bracelet**
    navy blue skirt suit
    white notched-collar blouse
    sheer panty hose
    navy slingback pumps
    two thin gold link bracelets

❀ **coral earrings**
❀ **coral bangle bracelet**
    black short wool shift
    black sheer panty hose
    black and bone Chanel-style pumps
    black leather bag

❀ **coral pin**
    gray pantsuit
    gray ribbed trouser socks
    black suede loafers
    gold earrings
    gold neck chain
    black Bugatti bag

❀ **coral Victorian branch pin**
❀ **coral bangle bracelet**
    black mid-calf linen shift
    black Chanel-style flats
    small gold Victorian earrings
    black patent leather envelope bag

❁ **coral branch pin** fastened
   to side of turtleneck
black short-sleeved mock turtleneck
   sweater
black mid-calf pleated skirt
black panty hose
black high-heeled loafers

❁ **coral earrings**
❁ **coral necklace**
black mid-calf linen dress
black alligator-patterned sandals
two gold bangle bracelets

❁ **coral earrings**
black skirt suit
white V-necked silk blouse
black sheer panty hose
black patent leather slingback shoes
black Chanel-style bag

COWBOY BOOTS

The first cowboy boots were plain leather with square toes and flat heels. The proportions began to change to meet the needs of a man who spent his day driving a herd of cattle from the plains of Texas to the railroad depots of Kansas. The heel rose in height to keep it from slipping out of the stirrup. The toe narrowed, to allow the foot to slip out easily if the cowboy fell off his horse. Topstitching was added to prevent the leather from buckling with water damage.

Cowboys became the first American cultural icons, and their style a symbol of self-reliance, strength, and independence. With the arrival of rodeo shows and movie cowboys such as Roy Rogers, cowboy boots became increasingly elaborate. Once made from a single plain leather, the boot blossomed with patterns and design. Cowboy boots became a canvas for tooling and stenciling, overlaid with exotic leathers and bursting with color.

A good pair of cowboy boots provides a splash of independence in any closet. A pair of black stenciled boots peeking out from the pants cuff takes the edge off a tailored black pantsuit, while the same boots with a flowered slip dress adds a touch of attitude.

Cowboy boot devotees insist that custom-made boots are the only way to get a proper fit. The narrow toes and high instep of cowboy boots make it difficult, but not impossible, to get a comfortable fit out of a box. If you're purchasing a cowboy boot, give yourself plenty of time and be prepared to try on dozens of styles from different of manufacturers (think blue jeans) to find the best fit for your foot. When you step into the right ones, your feet will know it immediately. Start with a pair in black and if you find that you reach for them frequently, expand to a pair of brown, red, or mixed leather patterns. Just as they do for the cowboy on the cattle trail, they will keep your feet safe and dry for years.

H o w   t o   W e a r
C o w b o y   B o o t s

❀ **black cowboy boots**
   black crew-neck sweater
   black pants
   red small cherry Bakelite pin on
      shoulder
   black tote bag or backpack

❀ **black cowboy boots**
   black pantsuit
   camel cashmere crew-neck sweater
   wooden horse-head pin on lapel
   black backpack

❀ **black or brown cowboy boots**
   off-white sweater set
   charcoal gray knit skirt
   small gold hoop earrings

❀ **red cowboy boots**
   white T-shirt
   black long jumper
   black Bakelite earrings
   black tote bag

❀ **black cowboy boots**
   off-white notched-collar shirt
   navy blazer
   blue jeans
   horse-head pin on blazer lapel
   black backpack or tote bag

❀ **brown lizard cowboy boots**
   bone linen shirt
   brown suede pants
   pearl stud earrings
   gold chain-link bracelet

❀ **red or black cowboy boots**
   white T-shirt
   black and white long slip dress
   pearl stud earrings
   red Bakelite bracelet

COWBOY HAT

Kansas, 1865. John B. Stetson watched in amazement as the throngs of cattle were herded on to trains by lean, tanned cowhands on horseback. As the cowboys worked tirelessly in all weather, the eastern hatmaker recognized the business opportunity that had led him out west. Setting up his equipment, Stetson shaped felt into a hat with a tall crown and full brim, headgear designed to protect the cowboy from the scorching heat and drenching rains of the Chisholm cattle trails. His hat could also double as a water carrier for dusty cowboys and their thirsty horses (which is how it got the nickname of ten-gallon hat).

The Stetson became an emblem of the American West. When cowboy crooners such as Tom Mix and Tex Ritter sparked a national passion for anything western,

How to Wear a Cowboy Hat

❀ **black cowboy hat**
   white sleeveless T-shirt
   blue jeans
   black cowboy boots

❀ **black cowboy hat**
   white cotton shirt
   blue denim short jacket
   blue jeans
   black cowboy boots

❀ **brown cowboy hat**
   white T-shirt
   bone jeans
   brown and tan cowboy boots

❀ **bone cowboy hat**
   white tank top
   prairie skirt
   white ballet flats

❀ **black cowboy hat**
   black cowboy shirt
   black tight jeans
   red cowboy boots

the cowboy hat became popular street wear in many parts of the country. It is one of the few motif accessories that looks best in context. Walk down a street almost anywhere in Texas, and you'll see people wearing cowboy hats with enviable style and grace. Take the same hat across the Mississippi and you'll look like a contestant from a traveling rodeo. If you live someplace where you might be riding a horse anytime soon, a Stetson can give an extra kick to your wardrobe. If not, save the hat for trips to big sky country or the occasional square dance.

CUFF BRACELET

This broad, snug bracelet is one of the fashion stylist's best-kept secrets. Two to four inches wide, it is usually made of molded metal or chunky multiple

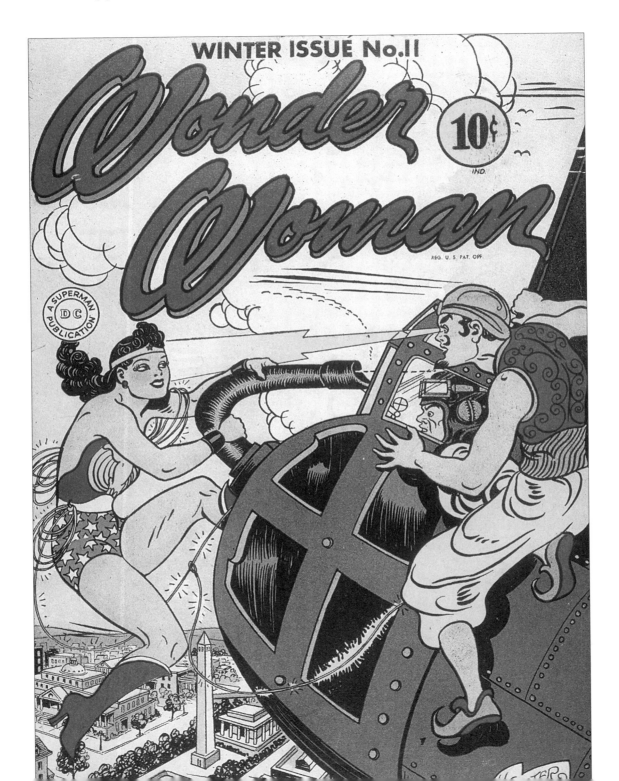

strands of pearls. A cuff bracelet like the classic molded metal cuff of Robert Lee Morris "anchors" the line of your clothes. More assertive than flexible bracelets, cuff bracelets provide balance and focus for sleeveless styles.

How to Wear a Cuff Bracelet

✿ **silver cuff bracelet**
   black long linen shift
   black flats
   silver hoop earrings
   black backpack

✿ **silver cuff bracelet**
   black short-sleeved mock turtleneck
   black skinny pants
   black suede mules

✿ **silver cuff bracelets**
   red short linen shift
   black and tan slingback shoes
   small silver hoop earrings
   black alligator tote bag

✿ **chunky pearl cuff bracelet**
   white T-shirt
   denim overalls
   white high-heeled platform sneakers

✿ **chunky pearl cuff bracelet**
   white sleeveless linen vest
   navy-and-white polka-dot
      mid-calf skirt

navy ballet flats
small pearl stud earrings

✿ **chunky pearl cuff bracelet**
   white long linen shift
   black and white Chanel-style flats
   pearl stud earrings

✿ **chunky pearl cuff bracelet**
   flowered long slip dress
   black and white Chanel-style flats
   pearl stud earrings

CUFF LINKS

Men have worn cuff links for over 300 years, in styles that have ranged from utilitarian to fabulous. Women first snapped on a pair of cuff links at the turn of the century when they traded in elaborate dresses for simple shirtwaists and long slim skirts.

Cuff links today are a subtle way of adding sparkle and expressing personality. People have to get close to catch a glimpse of a cuff as it peeks out of a jacket. There is a dazzling assortment of both vintage and contemporary cuff links available at prices to suit any budget. You will find them in gold, silver, enamel, or studded with jewels in styles that range from sporty to formal. The only limit—they can be worn only on shirts with French cuffs.

How to Wear Cuff Links

✿ **gold antique cuff links**
   white overshirt
   black mid-calf skirt
   black opaque panty hose
   black lace-up granny boots
   pearl stud earrings

✿ **jeweled cuff links**
   gray flannel suit
   white cotton shirt
   red cashmere sweater tied around
      shoulders
   gray ribbed trousers socks
   black high-heeled loafers
   gold earrings
   black bag

✿ **pearl stud cuff links**
   black pantsuit
   pale blue shirt
   black ankle-boots
   black nylon backpack

✿ **vintage equestrian-style cuff links**
   brown skirt suit
   off-white silk shirt
   brown opaque panty hose
   brown suede high-heeled loafers
   brown alligator Bugatti bag

✿ **rhinestone cluster cuff links**
   black velvet skirt suit
   white satin shirt
   black sheer panty hose
   black satin slingback pumps
   ruby and diamond earrings
   red minaudière or evening bag

CUMMERBUND

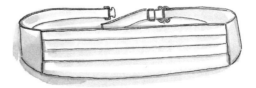

On a hot August night in 1903 in New Delhi, an English officer was sweltering in his three-piece evening suit. His eye fell on the manservant on the porch comfortably sitting in his Kamerband, or loincloth. The loosely pleated cloth gave the officer a novel idea. He took off his jacket and vest and arranged a length of black silk to cover his waist. The new style was elegant and mercifully cooler than the traditional formal attire. Now called a cummerbund, the pleated silk belt has become an established part of men's evening wear.

Over the years, women have adopted the belt for impact and style. The wide belt flatters a slim or straight body silhouette. As a female accessory, a cummerbund shapes the waist, creating an instant tongue-in-cheek style with its masculine look. If you are short-waisted, fasten the cummerbund lower on the waist, slightly higher if you are long-waisted.

If you can't find a cummerbund in the accessories department, look in the men's or boys' section. Black, white, red, or mini-geometrics called "wedding prints" are common. A more interesting selection will be found in flea markets and vintage clothing stores including plaids, paisleys, and madras in cottons and Indian tussah silks. To make your own cummerbund sash wrap an oblong scarf around your waist and tuck in the ends.

How to Wear a Cummerbund

❀ **red silk cummerbund**
  white tuxedo shirt
  black wool pants
  red and black Mickey Mouse socks
  black patent leather tuxedo loafers
  small rhinestone earrings
  rhinestone cuff links

❀ **red plaid vintage cummerbund**
  white linen shirt with rolled-up
    sleeves
  white linen pants
  white short socks
  red platform sandals
  straw tote bag trimmed with
    a cherry corsage

❀ **red-and-blue madras cummerbund**
  light blue denim shirt
  red oversized V-necked cardigan
  khaki pleated pants
  white socks
  red loafers
  tiny gold hoop earrings

❀ **turquoise satin cummerbund**
  fuchsia velvet hair bow
  white charmeuse jewel-neck blouse
  black short knit cardigan
  gray flannel pants
  gray textured dress socks
  black velvet evening pumps
  small pearl drop earrings
  fuchsia and turquoise rhinestone
    bracelet

❀ **black and silver "wedding" cummerbund**
  gray knit crew-neck top
  black ankle-length knit skirt or pants
  black opaque panty hose
  black suede high-heeled loafers

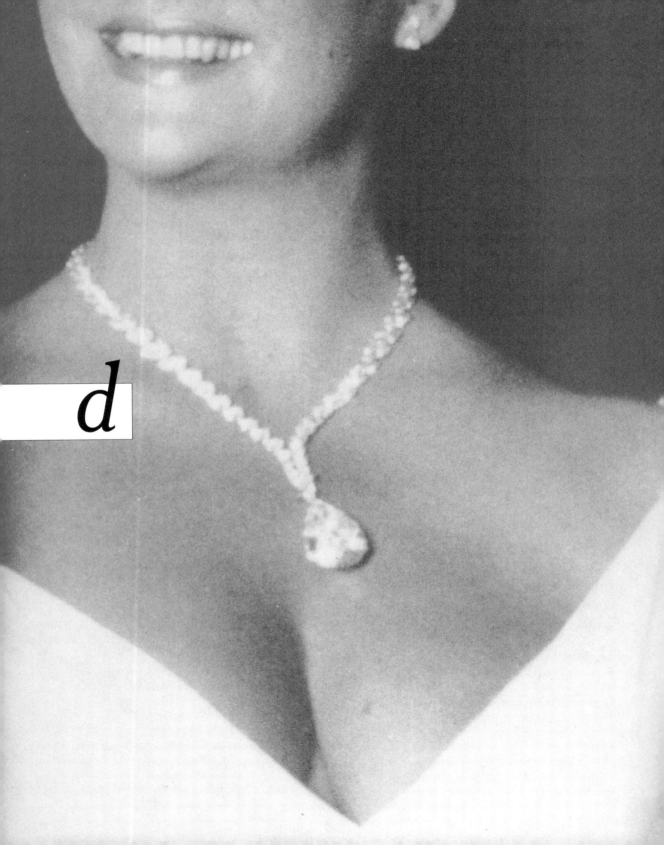

d

DERBY

The Earl of Derby was an 18th-century horseman who created a hat with a rounded crown and stiff brim to protect riders if they fell off their mounts. In the 1860s, William Bowler designed a version which soon became known as the bowler. For men it replaced the far more formal top hat. For women the brim was flattened for a witty, casual look.

You can still find genuine English derbies in flea markets and antique shops, as well as new hats in men's stores. Women's felt derbies are usually softer and lighter than traditional men's hats. Don't take this hat too seriously; wear it with a sense of humor and equally assertive accessories such as a string of large amber beads, oversized men's vests, vintage ties, and full pants.

A small black bowler was the hat of choice for cosmetic titan Helena Rubinstein. Tiny in stature with an ink black chignon, Madame Rubinstein paired her bowler with coats from Balenciaga and Dior, pleased that the tall crown added inches to her height. Usually made only in black, bowlers are hats with attitude, dominating the focus rather than creating balance.

How to Wear a Derby

✿ **black derby**
black and brown riding boots
black vintage men's wool coat

✿ **black derby**
black knee-high leather boots
red coat with black velvet collar

✿ **black derby**
gray wool steamer coat
large paisley shawl worn over the
shoulders

✿ **black derby**
white peasant overshirt
print mid-calf skirt
black cowboy boots
string of amber beads

✿ **black derby**
white peasant overskirt
black wool men's vest
drawstring pants
black oxfords

✿ **gray derby**
off-white silk shirt
gray pin-striped trousers
black high-heeled oxfords
loosely knotted men's vintage tie
pearl earrings

DIAMONDS

Blue, white, and perfect, diamonds have been the symbol of wealth, luxury, and love for centuries. Legend holds that a diamond enhances a husband's passion for a wife—a belief that led to the gem becoming the symbol of betrothal.

Diamonds are more than symbols—much more. They flatter every combination of skin, eye, and hair color. Diamonds radiate an icy sparkle that looks wonderful with both tailored and dressy styles. These gems generously share their brilliance, adding light and movement. They can have their greatest impact around the face. Even a tiny diamond on a chain or small diamond studs add significant yet subtle sparkle.

Diamonds are valued both for their fire (the rainbow of colors deep in the stone) and brilliance (their sparkle or liveliness). Fire and brilliance are in inverse proportion to each other. When a diamond is cut into facets (edges) the jeweler tries to balance both aspects.

Since the end of World War I, most diamonds have been styled with the brilliant cut. Marcel Tolkowsky, the Belgian-born jeweler, developed the modern cut with 58 facets for maximum fire and brilliance. Jewels designed before 1919 will probably be made in the old mine (round) or old European (square) cuts. While these styles lack brilliance, they can have an extraordinary fire. Diamonds

that date from the 15th to 17th centuries will frequently be the flat rose cut. A faceted diamond with a flat base, it looks like an unfolding rosebud.

Diamonds are used successfully in a variety of supporting roles. Pavé diamonds use tiny chips to cover a gold surface, producing an elegant yet affordable sparkle. Tiny diamonds that are measured in points rather then carats can surround a less expensive gem to create a particularly flattering piece of jewelry. For example, a garnet center casts a rosy glow on the skin, while the tiny diamonds around it reflect light.

How to Wear Diamonds

❁ **diamond stud earrings**
   gray pin-striped pantsuit
   white lace bodysuit
   gray opaque trouser socks

black high-heeled suede loafers
black leather bag

❁ **pearl and diamond cluster earrings**
❁ **old mine-cut diamond ring**
   deep red velvet shift
   black sheer panty hose
   black high-heeled satin sandals

❁ **gold and diamond bangle bracelet**
   navy crepe coatdress
   navy sheer panty hose
   navy pumps
   coral and gold earrings
   navy Chanel bag

❁ **diamond pavé earrings**
   red wool skirt suit
   black panty hose
   black patent leather pumps
   gold bangle bracelets
   black envelope bag

THE GREAT IMPOSTORS

Diamonds are probably the most expensive accessory a woman can own. For centuries people have looked for substitutes to provide a diamond's fire and brilliance. Glass will also sparkle, but without a diamond's fire. Rhinestones are glass or rock crystal with foil backing to generate a rainbow of colors. After time, the foil disintegrates and the glass looks dull and spotty.

The most successful diamond substitute to date is cubic zirconium, a man-made jewel. A well-designed piece can easily pass for the real thing. But even if they look genuine, there are many women who cherish the sense of self-worth that comes from wearing the genuine article.

❂ **pearl and diamond earrings**
white chiffon dress
silver sandals

❂ **diamond solitaire on chain**
black stretchy velvet dress
black tights
black ankle-boots

❂ **diamond cocktail ring**
black gabardine pantsuit
white cashmere T-shirt
black suede wedge shoes
diamond stud earrings

❂ **diamond stud earrings**
white silk cropped turtleneck
black silk Chinese jacket
black mid-calf knit skirt
black tights
black Chanel-style flats
black nylon tote bag

❂ **pavé diamond earrings**
❂ **gold and diamond bangle bracelet**
black turtleneck sweater
black-and-white-checked short skirt
black thin opaque panty hose
black chunky pumps

❂ **diamond stud earrings**
red sweatband
navy sweatshirt
white running shorts
white running shoes

DOC MARTENS

It is hard to think of another shoe that has successfully gone through such an image makeover as the Doc Martens. They were first designed at the end of World War II by a German physician to make walking easier while his leg healed from a skiing injury. Dark, bulky, and somber, they were destined to remain anonymous orthopedic shoes when an enterprising English shoe manufacturer decided they would be the perfect footwear for the North Country working man. However, the real audience turned out to be not the British laborer, but the rising gangs of alienated English skinheads. These angry and violent young men saw Doc Martens as the perfect shoe with which to attack (both metaphorically and physically) the British bourgeoisie. It didn't work out as they planned. Doc Martens were enthusiastically adopted by well-behaved university students who are delighted by the comfortable, practical shoe with a rebellious subtext.

Worn today by students around the world, Doc Martens are the perfect finish for casual jeans and tough black leather, but still can take the fussiness out of skirts and jumpers. Black and Doc Martens are practically synonymous, but if you love the way they look and feel, try a pair in bright red or green. On a cold, wet day they let you "own" the weather.

H o w t o W e a r
D o c M a r t e n s

❂ **black Doc Martens**
  white T-shirt
  blue denim overalls
  white crew socks
  Indian print oblong scarf slung
    around neck

❂ **black Doc Martens**
  white T-shirt
  black leather jacket
  black leggings
  diamond stud earrings

❂ **black Doc Martens**
  white T-shirt
  gray oversized V-necked sweater
  gray print mid-calf skirt
  white crew socks

❂ **black Doc Martens**
  white fisherman's sweater
  black-and-red buffalo-check
    flannel skirt
  black tights
  pearl stud earrings

❂ **black Doc Martens**
  flowered short summer dress
  white socks
  small gold hoop earrings

DUFFEL BAG

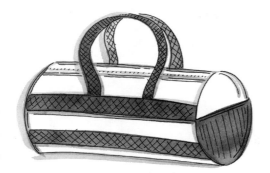

Originally the soldier's duffel bag was a cylindrical canvas bag with a drawstring top that folded over and locked into a clamp. It was sturdy and light (at least when empty) and had a seemingly inexhaustible capacity to hold everything.

The duffel is an oversized sport sac that is used regularly as a weekend or gym bag. It's too big to serve as a purse, but is a great piece of casual luggage.

e

EARRINGS

There are few accessories that can have as much effect on the face as a pair of earrings. Round or square, plain or fancy, earrings bring light, color, and movement to the face. They can have more impact than makeup, bringing out your best features and correcting less than perfect ones. For example, large earrings make a nose look smaller, silver hoops cool down a ruddy complexion, and a pair of gold button earrings warm up winter-pale skin tones.

Earrings are the perfect finish to a look, adding balance, polish, and personality. Clean-cut, classic, gold dome- or "shrimp"-style earrings project quiet professionalism; pearl drops are feminine and flirtatious; colorful vintage Bakelite tell a room that talking to you will never be boring.

The only problem with earrings is choosing which ones to wear. Some styles, like small diamonds, are appropriate with everything from bathing suits to ball gowns. Most women are flattered by a wide range of sizes, styles, and

shapes. In general, wide earrings broaden a narrow face, drop and oval earrings balance a full face, and cluster shapes add fullness to a long face.

There are advantages and disadvantages to both pierced earrings, which have been around since the time of the pharaohs, and screw-back or clip-on earrings, a 19th-century innovation. Pierced styles fit smoothly into the earlobe, and are less likely to be lost. On the downside, they need to be worn almost constantly to prevent the holes in the ear from closing; the holes can become infected; and larger styles can stretch the lobes unattractively. Screwback earrings can be more difficult to position on the ear and painful to wear, and tend to fall off or are forgotten when taken off at the telephone. All of these issues sound a lot worse than they are, and the choice of backing is a personal decision.

Unlike shoes, bags, and hats, earrings never go out of fashion. Start with universal styles such as pearls, diamond studs, and small hoops in gold or silver. As you try on different styles and sizes you will develop an eye for those that are the most flattering to your face. Look for these styles in a range of materials including ivory, amber, coral, gemstones, Bakelite, and pearls for an earring collection that you will enjoy for a lifetime.

H o w   t o   W e a r
E a r r i n g s

✿ **mabe pearl earrings**
   white silk shirt
   red boucle jacket
   black short skirt
   black sheer panty hose
   black patent leather pumps
   24-inch gold chain

✿ **pearl stud earrings**
   blue-and-white-striped T-shirt
   white linen pants
   white patent leather driving shoes
   gold chain bracelets
   straw bag with a corsage of cherries

✿ **diamond stud earrings**
   black bikini
   black patent leather thong sandals

TEN TIPS FOR WEARING EARRINGS

1. Slender, petite women need airy shapes.
2. Larger earrings make the nose look smaller.
3. Dome earrings de-emphasize a prominent nose.
4. Pearls, turquoise, rubies, coral, and garnets are flattering on brunettes.
5. Emeralds, jade, sapphire, amethyst, silver, platinum, and pale gold look especially good on redheads.
6. Multicolored earrings brighten the complexion.
7. The red glow of rubies and garnets, and the fire of diamonds are flattering to all complexions.
8. If your face is round, choose oval, asymmetrical, or angular shapes rather than round earrings.
9. Long faces benefit from broad-shaped earrings.
10. Avoid drop earrings if you have a long face or a short neck.

❂ **coral earrings**
 navy skirt suit
 off-white silk shirt
 navy or bone sheer panty hose
 navy slingback pumps
 24-inch rope of pearls
 double-strand pearl bracelet
 navy Bugatti bag

❂ **red Bakelite earrings**
 navy linen pantsuit
 white T-shirt
 navy-and-white polka-dot socks
 navy loafers
 red Bakelite cuff bracelet

❂ **gold earrings**
 men's tailored cotton shirt
 navy blazer
 blue jeans
 navy argyle socks
 brown suede loafers
 brown Kelly bag

EMERALDS

Emeralds, the most prized jewels of ancient civilizations, were originally dug out of a mine named after Cleopatra. The deep, dark grass-green color has long been linked with magical powers that range from fidelity to snake bite protection. For hundreds of years the finest gemstones came from the dark, violent Colombian emerald mines.

Unlike diamonds, where clarity and perfection are essential, inclusions and flaws are acceptable components of fine emeralds, and, in fact, give the stone depth and character. As the rarest and most expensive of all gemstones, the glorious green deepens as the stone increases in size.

The finest stones are step cut with a flat top and mitered corners, a shape known as the emerald cut. Lesser stones are smoothed into beads or polished into cabochon beads and domes. Badly flawed stones are frequently carved with designs.

Emeralds look spectacular combined with pearls, rubies, and diamonds. They look beautiful with elegant daytime clothes as well as luxurious evening fabrics such as velvet, Indian silk, and filmy chiffon.

How to Wear Emeralds

❂ **emerald and pearl earrings**
  black velvet shift
  black sheer panty hose
  black satin slingback spike shoes
  gold minaudière

❂ **emerald cabochon earrings**
❂ **diamond and emerald bracelet**
  black satin-trimmed wool
    cocktail dress
  black sheer panty hose
  black satin high-heeled pumps
  black suede envelope bag with gold
    clasp

❂ **gold, emerald, and ruby necklace**
  beige floor-length silk evening dress
  pale sheer panty hose
  beige silk pumps
  ruby cabochon earrings

❂ **emerald and diamond ring**
  white short-sleeved cashmere
    crew-neck sweater
  black paillette-trimmed jacket with
    white chevron stripes
  white wool trousers
  white Chanel flats with gold toes

❂ **emerald and diamond necklace**
  fuchsia floor-length faille
    evening dress
  fuchsia, gold, and green embroidered
    bolero jacket
  pale sheer panty hose
  fuchsia satin high-heeled sandals
  diamond earrings
  pale gold brocade satin envelope bag
    with jeweled clasp

ENVELOPE BAG

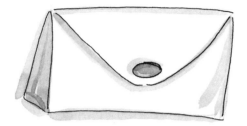

Until the 1920s, handbags were little drawstring sacks hung modestly over the wrist. They worked well as long as women needed only to carry a few dainty items: a lace hankie, a tiny vial of cologne, perhaps a few coins. As their world expanded, women needed a new type of bag to carry their new necessities. The flat hard envelope-shaped bag tucked smartly under the arm was the perfect carrier for the modern basics in the 1930s—a compact, a cigarette case, and a lighter.

By current standards the envelope bag is on the small side, but it can still be the perfect touch of elegance with a suit or dress.

The envelope bag works beautifully as an occasional bag—an elegant way to carry a few essentials when you're going to specific event (i.e., the theater, dinner, or a party) rather than setting out for a day's activities. Larger envelopes (10 to 12 inches) work best with daytime clothes, while smaller ones (6 to 8 inches) are perfect for dressier clothes. Start with a smooth or patent leather black envelope. If you feel the shape works for you, look for the envelope in suede, straw, or crocodile patterned leathers. Keep an eye out for 1940s-style envelopes made from colorful wooden beads if you like the feel and look of a bag tucked under your arm.

How to Wear an Envelope Bag

❂ **black patent leather envelope bag**
 red skirt suit
 white silk shirt or black-and-white-
  plaid silk shirt
 black sheer panty hose
 black patent leather shoes
 gold and pearl earrings
 baroque pearl necklace

CARRY AN ENVELOPE BAG WITH . . .

- **flat fabric coats (it can damage fur coats under the arm).**
- **three-quarter-length coats for a 1930s look with a straight column skirt and a beret.**
- **short suit coats. Although the coat has volume, the movement will not overwhelm the bag as much as a camel polo coat.**
- **a full swing skirt with a narrow top and a cinch belt for a 1950s look.**

✿ **bone envelope bag**
  peach silk skirt suit
  bone silk shirt
  bone panty hose
  bone leather pumps
  pearl or opal earrings

✿ **silver envelope bag**
  white chiffon dress
  silver high-heeled sandals
  diamond earrings
  pearl necklace

✿ **brown suede envelope bag**
  camel skirt suit
  brown cashmere shell
  brown ribbed opaque panty hose
  brown alligator pumps
  antique gold earrings
  gold chain link bracelet

✿ **black patent leather envelope bag**
  yellow silk skirt suit
  bone sheer panty hose
  black patent leather shoes
  mabe pearl earrings
  double-strand pearl bracelet

✿ **black envelope bag**
  black short linen shift
  black patent leather slingback pumps
  pearl necklace
  black straw hat

ESPADRILLES

If ever there was a shoe synonymous with summer, it is the espadrille. This rope-soled, canvas slip-on was worn by French fishermen for centuries. In the 1920s vacationers began to flood the south of France and were charmed by the style and comfort of the casual shoe. One word of advice: espadrilles are not especially sturdy, and tend to disintegrate after a summer by the sea.

How to Wear Espadrilles

✿ **pink-checked espadrilles**
  white T-shirt
  white duck pants
  pearl stud earrings
  straw bag with pink and white flowers
    pinned to its side

✿ **red espadrilles**
  blue-and-white-striped shirt
  white shorts
  small gold hoop earrings
  red and blue flowered bag

❀ **red espadrilles**
   white-and-blue-striped T-shirt
   navy linen pants
   navy Bugatti bag
   large gold hoop earrings

❀ **black espadrilles**
   black and white slip dress
   pearl stud earrings
   small black linen shoulder bag
      worn across the chest

❀ **white espadrilles**
   white tank top
   gauzy long skirt
   medium gold hoop earrings

❀ **black espadrilles**
   white polo shirt
   black-and-white-checked pants
   pearl earrings

EYEGLASSES

The origins of eyeglasses are a bit a hazy, but most fashion historians agree that they appeared simultaneously in Italy and China in the 13th century. Because most people could neither read nor owned books, wearing glasses became a symbol of wisdom and wealth. For centuries glasses were made of heavy bone, horn, or ivory frames with equally weighty glass lenses. Too heavy to be worn comfortably for more than a few hours, glasses were strictly a utilitarian item. The introduction of lightweight plastic frames and lenses turned glasses into a fashion imperative.

Glasses are not a shy accessory. They're out there, shaping your face, framing your eyes, making a statement. Choosing the ultimate frame requires a balance of shape, color, material, and weight. When you first walk into an optometrist's shop, there are literally dozens of frames stacked on the shelves and nestled in cabinets. So many choices, so little time. Start with the weight. If you're slim and small-boned, look for delicate frames; thicker and weightier frames would be a better choice if you have a heavier build.

Now consider color and material. Unless you want to be known as "the girl with the glasses," don't wear frames that are obviously darker than your hair. Warm blond, red, and medium brown hair color is flattered by frames in gold or warm shades of tortoiseshell. Gray, white, black, and ashy blond hair goes beautifully with silver or the grayed tones of tortoiseshell.

At this point it's time to narrow down selections by size. The top edge of the frames should cover your eyebrows, while the bottom rim should at least hit the cheekbone. What is left is a reasonable selection of glasses in different shapes. Keep trying them on until you and the frames are one.

If you wear glasses just for reading you'll probably want a basic, albeit flattering pair. If you wear them all the time, you might consider having several pairs in different styles and colors. A varied wardrobe of glasses could include a pair in metal, another in tortoiseshell, and a third in a colorful frame or interesting shape.

H o w   t o   W e a r
E y e g l a s s e s

✿ **red-framed round glasses**
　 red short-sleeved T-shirt
　 white cotton overalls
　 white high-top sneakers

✿ **round gold wire-rimmed glasses**
　 bone linen shirt
　 brown tweed jacket
　 brown mid-calf suede skirt
　 brown cowboy boots
　 antique gold earrings
　 lace-trimmed handkerchief
　 　 in pocket of jacket

✿ **thin tortoiseshell frames**
　 black linen dress
　 black high-heeled sandals
　 pearl earrings
　 black straw tote bag

✿ **black plastic-framed glasses**
　 white cotton shirt
　 perfectly cut blue jeans
　 black cowboy boots
　 silver "bean" earrings
　 black nylon tote bag

✿ **white harlequin-framed glasses**
　 white happy-face T-shirt
　 red-and-white-bandanna-print
　 　 mid-calf skirt
　 white ballet flats
　 red Bakelite bangle bracelet

✿ **black-framed glasses**
　 black cashmere mock turtleneck
　 black cigarette pants
　 black ankle-boots
　 silver earrings
　 silver cuff bracelet

f

FAIR ISLE

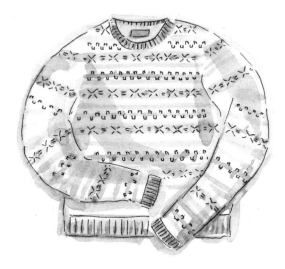

A multicolored geometric pattern, Fair Isle originated in the Shetland Isles of Scotland. This pattern jumped from a local style to a staple of Anglo-American chic in the 1920s when the Prince of Wales chose Fair Isle sweaters for his beloved golf game. Since that time it has been a preppy constant paired with tweeds, corduroys, and khakis. Fair Isle is both a sporty and dainty pattern, adding muted color to tailored or rugged clothing. You'll find it lavished on sweaters, hats, vests, scarves, and gloves.

How to Wear Fair Isle

✿ **Fair Isle crew-neck sweater**
  white turtleneck
  khaki pants
  off-white cashmere socks
  tan driving shoes
  pearl stud earrings
  navy peacoat

✿ **Fair Isle vest**
  blue oxford shirt
  tan corduroy pants
  navy thick socks
  alligator-patterned brown loafers
  small gold hoop earrings
  brown backpack

✿ **Fair Isle knit cap**
  brown corduroy pants
  oatmeal chunky socks
  brown hiking boots
  small antique gold earrings
  camel polo coat
  cranberry cashmere scarf
  pigskin gloves

✿ **Fair Isle sweater**
  brown knit skirt
  brown riding boots
  tiny pearl stud earrings
  shearling jacket
  brown backpack

FEATHERS

There are few accessories as feminine as feathers—but along with bustles and frock coats, feathers have practically vanished from the fashion radar screen. You will still find feathers on a few hats and handbags, or made into a boa or collar. Properly used, feathers are intensely flattering. Near the face they soften features and seemingly erase lines.

Feathers are near the top of the short list of accessories that open communication. There is something playful about feathers that encourages people to approach you—always helpful when you are going to a party alone. To many men, feathers are provocative; they think you are flirting without saying a word.

Most of the feathered accessories are made of two feather varieties: ostrich and marabou. Ostrich feathers are soft, wide, and graceful plumes that vary from 1 to 12 inches long. Naturally white or black, they can be dyed to any imaginable shade. The shorter and fluffier marabou feathers were originally from the egret. When these birds faced extinction due to a worldwide passion for feathers, naturalists successfully lobbied for protective legislation. No longer able to import egret, milliners have turned to turkey feathers for a similar look.

How to Wear Feathers

❂ **black feathered bag**
  black velvet pantsuit
  black sheer trouser socks
  black high-heeled satin sandals
  diamond stud earrings

❂ **black feather boa**
  black mid-calf crepe slip dress
  black sheer panty hose
  black satin slingback shoes
  diamond stud earrings
  black satin envelope bag

✪ **black feather bow** holding a ponytail

    black crew-neck sweater

    black wool pants

    black ribbed trouser socks

    black ballet flats

    pearl stud earrings

✪ **red feathered bag**

    white turtleneck

    black miniskirt

    black tights

    black suede loafers

    black and red Bakelite earrings

    black and white vintage men's
       tweed coat

FEDORA

This soft-brimmed felt hat is arguably the queen of headgear. A popular men's hat of the 1900s, it was actually named for a woman—the heroine of a play by the French writer Victorian Sardou. The part was written for Sarah Bernhardt, and both the play and the hat were the rage of 19th-century Paris. Men wore it tilted over one eye, while women often added a veil or feather.

This hat loves women of all shapes, ages, and sizes. The brim flatters noses big and small, as it makes the eyes appear deep and passionate. The soft brim and crown can be shaped to suit individual features. Some women look best with the brim raised in front. Others shine with the front tilted down over one eye and the back lifted up. This is a hat to play with.

How to Wear a Fedora

✪ **tan fedora**

    blue denim shirt

    white popcorn-stitch sweater

    gabardine pants

    hiking boots

    gold earrings

    gold chain bracelets

    shearling coat

✿ **black fedora**
   black boots
   Hopi silver earrings
   black and white men's vintage overcoat

✿ **tan fedora**
   black crew-neck sweater
   black pants
   brown and black riding boots
   silver earrings
   silver cuff bracelet
   tan trench coat
   black tote bag

✿ **black fedora**
   off-white turtleneck
   gray pants
   gray and black argyle socks
   black suede loafers
   black pearl earrings
   black cashmere wrap coat

FISHNET STOCKINGS

There are accessories and then there are accessories with attitude. Fishnet stockings are not subtle hosiery; they demand attention and they usually get it. They were designed for situations where hose needed to be both tight and flexible. They were a favorite among dancers who required hosiery with a smooth tight fit and enough flexibility for high kicks and low bends. These stockings were too sexy to remain only on stage, and eventually entered mainstream fashion. Fishnet panty hose crank up a plain black wool shift into black-tie status. Wear them with solids rather than patterns and check for runs. Torn fishnet stockings are only cool as a political statement.

How to Wear Fishnet Stockings

✿ **black fishnet stockings**
   black velvet shift
   3-inch black satin sandals
   diamond earrings
   black and gold minaudière

✿ **black fishnet stockings**
   black crew-neck sweater
   black mid-calf wool skirt
   black suede ballet flats
   silver hoop earrings
   silver cuff bracelet

✿ **black fishnet stockings**
   black wool suit with fitted
      jacket and short skirt
   black 3-inch suede heels
   diamond stud earrings
   black suede envelope bag

FLIGHT BAG

In the early days of air travel a flight was a special occasion. Men wore suits and women dressed up with pearls and white gloves. To commemorate the trip airlines gave their passengers canvas bags with side pockets. Inspired by the safari bag, the flight bag was designed to hold papers and books, as well as personal items for the often lengthy flight (it took 12 hours to fly from New York to Los Angeles).

Complimentary flight bags have disappeared along with traveling suits, white gloves, and recognizable airline food, but the style is still available in handbag and luggage departments. It is still an excellent bag, particularly if you are accompanied by children. A neutral color like black or tan will be practical while a bright yellow canvas will be much more fun.

This bag should be ready to work hard for you, so check out the zippers and seams. Look for solid construction and sturdy closures. While evaluating the merits of a flight bag, drape it over your shoulder to try it on. Make sure it hangs comfortably and is the appropriate size for you.

FLOWERS

Flowers as decoration probably began when a young Neolithic housewife stuck a bunch of wildflowers on her deerskin shirt. Beautiful, colorful, and intensely feminine, natural flowers are too fragile and seasonal to wear easily. In the late 18th century Italian and French craftsmen created artificial ones from silk and flowers became a fashion standard.

Generally flowers have been used on hats. Sometimes a single bloom is nestled on the side of a small straw hat. Large hats could be weighed down with dozens of big and small blossoms of every imaginable color. When hats shrank to the small tight cloche of the 1920s, flowers moved from the head to the chest. During that time, no outfit seemed quite complete without a bouquet of artificial flowers pinned to the shoulder. A few years later, Chanel created a flower classic by positioning a single white gardenia at the throat. During the 1930s and '40s, wearing a corsage of orchids on a suit, dress, or coat was considered a sign of elegance and high style.

Wearing flowers today, whether real or artificial, reveals a confident femininity in a time of often androgynous clothing. Like Chanel, some women choose to wear a certain flower as their signature. Others collect a variety for a range of occasions, making the floral accent their personal style. Eleanor Roosevelt pinned a large bouquet of orchids on the outside of her winter coat. And remember the sensation caused by Sharon Stone at the Academy Awards when she arrived wearing a minimal black T-shirt with a white gardenia pinned to her evening wrap?

How to Wear Flowers

❁ **white gardenia** pinned to jacket
  shoulder
  white collarless silk shirt
  black long wool jacket
  black-and-white-checked miniskirt
  black sheer panty hose
  black suede pumps
  pearl stud earrings

❁ **bunch of violets** at the neck
  lavender long-sleeved silk crew-neck
    sweater

  gray flannel pants
  black suede loafers
  pearl earrings
  black suede envelope bag

❁ **yellow sunflower hair clip**
  white mid-calf linen shift
  white slides
  small pearl drop earrings
  straw tote with yellow gingham bow

❁ **lily of the valley** worn on the lapel
  pale gray skirt suit
  white notched-collar silk shirt
  black sheer panty hose
  black patent leather slingback pumps
  pearl and gold earrings
  black Chanel bag

❁ **small nosegay of pink and
  white flowers** pinned to ribbon
    of straw hat
  white mid-calf linen shift
  white ballet flats
  small pearl drop earrings

❁ **big red satin rose** pinned to lapel
  white satin long-sleeved T-shirt
  black fitted wool jacket
  black-and-white-checked pants
  off-white trouser socks
  black suede Mary Jane pumps
  pearl stud earrings
  red and black Bakelite bracelet

✿ **one black, one red rose**
    pinned at neck
    red long-sleeved crew-neck sweater
    black mid-calf wool skirt
    black platform boots
    pearl stud earrings
    black polo coat
    red gloves

✿ **white gardenia** on black-and-white
    polka-dot bow barrette
    white T-shirt

    black slim linen pants
    black ballet flats
    pearl button earrings
    black Kelly bag

✿ **yellow sunflower** hair-bow clip
    white mid-calf linen sundress
    white varsity V-necked sweater
        with yellow and blue stripes
    white slip-on Keds
    blue-and-white-gingham tote bag

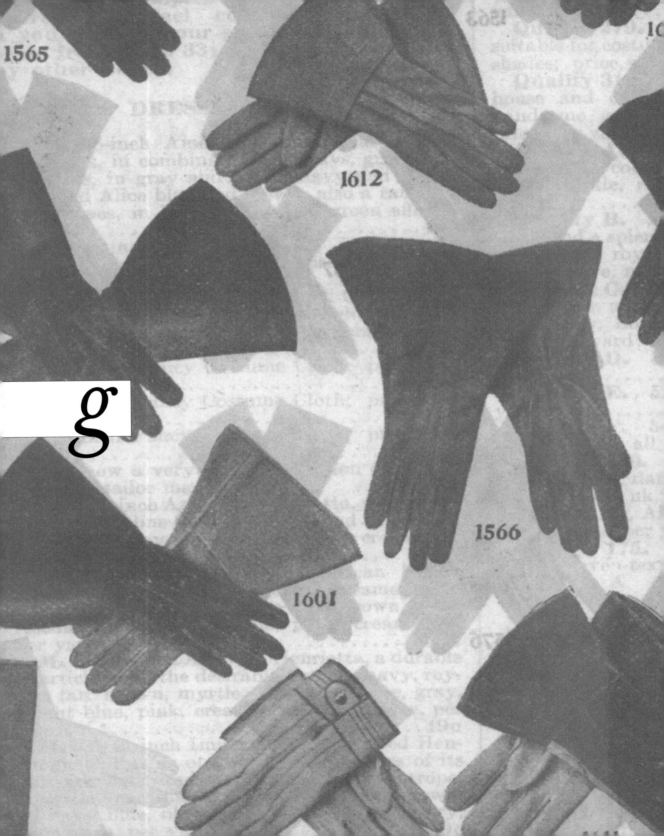

1565

1612

g

1566

1601

GARBO HAT
(AKA SLOUCH HAT, VAGABOND HAT)

This hat was first worn by Greta Garbo in the 1928 movie *A Woman of Affairs*. Created by Adrian, the great Hollywood designer, it was based on a slightly larger cloche hat of the 1920s. The Garbo was worn slanted on an angle and pulled down over the forehead. This asymmetrical style worked beautifully with the bias-cut clothing of the 1930s. In felt, straw, or wool it was, for a decade, the most popular hat in America.

While it is the hat that bears her name, the Garbo was not the only hat style inspired by the Swedish actress. Garbo had been a millinery model in Stockholm and she understood and enjoyed headgear. The hats that she wore in over 20 movies were not just unique, they were inherently flattering to a woman's face and body.

For the movie *Romance*, Adrian designed an ostrich feathered hat which

partially covered one eye. It was widely copied, as was the pillbox that Adrian created for Garbo to wear in the movie *As You Desire Me.* After seeing Garbo in a trim tight beret, women everywhere followed her style, tilting the beret over to one side and turning up the collar of their coat.

The modern Garbo hat has the same basic shape, but it is not as tight or severe. It is an excellent choice to top slim or bias-cut coats and dresses.

How to Wear a Garbo Hat

❂ **brown felt Garbo hat**
    brown leather boots
    caramel wool slim coat
    brown leather gloves
    brown suede envelope bag

❂ **straw Garbo hat**
    flowered mid-calf cotton dress
    bone ballet flats
    pearl stud earrings

❂ **black felt Garbo hat**
    black knee-high boots
    black and white slim tweed coat

❂ **black velvet Garbo hat**
    black opaque panty hose
    black high-heeled patent leather
       Mary Janes
    black bias-cut wool coat

GARNETS

Rich and intense, garnets have a dark brilliance found in no other gem. The birthstone of January, garnets share the complexion-enhancing characteristics of the other red-hued gems, rubies and coral.

Garnets look beautiful combined with gold, diamonds, and pearls. They look wonderful with navy, rich browns, and gray. Antique garnet jewelry was set in both silver or gold and looks beautiful with both metals.

How to Wear Garnets

❂ **pearl and garnet earrings**
    navy gabardine skirt suit
    white silk shirt
    pale sheer panty hose
    navy slingback pumps
    cameo pin
    navy shoulder bag on gold-tone chain

❂ **garnet and pearl earrings**
❂ **garnet bracelet**
    black velvet tank dress
    black sheer panty hose
    black high-heeled silk sandals
    black silk envelope bag

❂ **garnet earrings**
    cranberry crew-neck sweater
    gray flannel pants

BOHEMIAN GARNETS

Y ou will see numerous pieces described as Bohemian garnets. This region of the Czech Republic has been the center of garnet production since the 16th century. Bohemian style, a favorite with Victorians, uses numerous gems of different sizes to create elaborate yet delicate designs. According to legend, jewelry production was located on an island near Bohemia, and only authorized workers were allowed to set foot on it. Intruders were eliminated without mercy.

gray trouser socks
black suede loafers
black Bugatti bag

✿ **garnet brooch**
gray pantsuit
black quilted ballet flats
black ribbed trouser socks
pearl earrings
black Kelly bag

✿ **gold and garnet earrings**
navy linen coatdress
pale sheer panty hose
navy slingback pumps
pearl necklace
navy shoulder bag on gold chain

✿ **garnet and pearl bracelet**
navy linen pantsuit
white linen vest worn as blouse
navy flats
pearl earrings
navy shoulder bag

✿ **garnet cluster earrings**
✿ **garnet brooch on purse**
black wool crepe skirt suit
black sheer panty hose
black suede pumps
pearl necklace
black suede envelope bag

GLOVES

MY LADY'S GLOVE

Gloves are the aristocrats of accessories. Once worn only by kings, princes, and churchmen, they were the visible symbols of their owners' wealth and power. Their image endured for centuries, and carried over to a tradition that expected a woman to wear gloves for all occasions.

The sea change of social values that

THE LONG AND SHORT OF GLOVES

- SHORTY GLOVES are wrist-length styles with an opening on the side or center. Some shorties have small button or snap closures.
- SLIP-ON GLOVES extend 2 to 3 inches past the wrist, so that there is no gap between the gloves and the end of your sleeve.
- GAUNTLET GLOVES are designed with an insert that flares the glove above the wrist. These dramatic gloves can be decorated with fringes along the lower edge.
- MOUQUETAIRE are long formal gloves that often close with a long row of little buttons. Depending on the length, they can contain between 8 and 24 buttons.

All of these styles can be found in leather, cotton, wool, suede, and cashmere.

followed the 1960s included the end of the glove culture. Now worn primarily to keep warm and on rare formal occasions, a great-looking pair of gloves can still pack a fashion wallop. The right glove anchors the sleeve of a coat or jacket, providing an opportunity to express confidence and personality. For example, a pair of black slip-on kid gloves adds an elegant polish to a slim red wool coat; a short pigskin glove adds texture to a tan raincoat; at night a pair of long black lace gloves turns a simple black crepe tank dress into an event.

How to Wear Gloves

❂ **black leather slip-on gloves**
black boots
dark brown mink coat
black suede bag

❂ **tan driving gloves**
off-white cashmere turtleneck
green corduroy pants
brown hiking boots
brown canvas barn jacket
pearl stud earrings

❂ **red cashmere gloves**
black turtleneck
black wool pants
black cowboy boots
black and white vintage men's coat

❂ **tan pigskin gloves**
white turtleneck sweater
blue denim shirt
blue jeans
bluchers
gold knot earrings
brown tweed jacket

❂ **hot pink leather gloves**
pink Hermès-style scarf
black boots
gold earrings
black wool slim coat
black tote bag

❂ **heather Fair Isle knit gloves**
cranberry turtleneck
brown corduroy pants
brown boots
olive green quilted barn jacket
brown backpack

GOLD

We desire it. We've gone to war for it. We never feel we have enough. Ancient man linked gold to the sun and was convinced that the shiny stone was a source of great power. Soon this power was transformed to a perception of wealth. Theseus the Greek was the first ruler to mark gold with a specific value. During the Middle Ages, the science of alchemy focused on a single goal—to change lead to gold. Over the centuries, European armies destroyed the Inca and Maya civilizations to satisfy their hunger for gold. Blood, gore, and mysticism aside, we like to wear gold because it makes us look prettier. The honeyed light that gold reflects on skin and hair flatters everyone. Like a well-placed Hollywood key light, gold seems to highlight good features and blur lesser ones.

Pure gold is too soft to be used alone, and must be combined with other metals. The proportion of gold to base

metal yields the carat value. Gold mixed with copper has a pinkish cast; gold combined with nickel yields white-tone gold; classic yellow gold results from a combination of gold with silver. Pink gold around the face adds a bit of blush to yellow-based skin tones; white gold cools rough, reddened skin tones. Yellow gold flatters virtually every skin tone.

Depending on the style and weight, gold can be sporty, tailored, or dressy. A gold necklace, bracelet, and a pair of earrings are basics that never go out of style.

How to Wear Gold

✿ **gold dome earrings**
✿ **large gold pin** on shoulder
✿ **three thin gold bangle bracelets**
  tobacco brown wool skirt suit
  black mock turtleneck sweater
  brown sheer panty hose
  brown pumps

✿ **gold heart earrings**
✿ **20-inch gold chain**
✿ **gold and black enamel bangle bracelets**
  black linen pantsuit
  white silk shirt
  black suede loafers
  black Kelly bag

✿ **gold "shrimp" earrings**
✿ **gold and black enamel bangle bracelets**
✿ **gold wristwatch**
  black wool coatdress
  black or bone sheer panty hose
  black slingback pumps
  black Chanel bag

✿ **small gold hoop earrings**
✿ **one pearl and two gold bangle bracelets**
  black turtleneck
  black long jacket
  black-and-white-checked skirt
  black tights
  black suede chunky
    high-heeled loafers

✿ **gold and pearl earrings**
✿ **gold "San Marco" bracelet**
  navy short-sleeved skirt suit
  navy slingback pumps
  pale-toned sheer panty hose
  small navy shoulder bag

✿ **gold flower earrings**
  red wool skirt suit
  white shirt
  black sheer panty hose
  black pumps
  pearl bracelet
  small black shoulder bag

GOLD VOCABULARY LIST

- **24K**: pure gold.
- **14K**: 14 parts of gold to 10 parts of another metal.
- **18K**: 18 parts of gold to 6 parts of another metal.
- **GOLD PLATED**: thin covering of gold over silver.
- **FILLED GOLD**: base metal covered with thin sheet of gold that is between $1/10$ and $1/20$ the weight of the base metal.
- **ROLLED GOLD**: base metal covered with a thin sheet of gold that is between $1/30$ and $1/40$ the weight of the base metal.

GRANNY GLASSES (AKA BEN FRANKLIN GLASSES)

These wire-rim glasses have perched on many famous noses, from Joseph Stalin to John Lennon. A minimalist design, they are best with small-boned bodies and delicate features. The lenses can be round, rectangular, oval, or octagonal, but always smaller than those found in other styles of wire-rimmed frames (e.g., aviator glasses). The smaller proportions project a vintage, slightly quirky, casual style.

How to Wear Granny Glasses

✿ **granny glasses**
white long-sleeved T-shirt
Fair Isle vest
mid-calf denim skirt
granny boots
pearl stud earrings

✿ **granny glasses**
black bowler
white shirt
khaki baggy pants
black oxfords
vintage men's tie

✿ **granny glasses**
white overshirt
flowered mid-calf skirt
black ballet flats
string of amber beads

✿ **granny glasses**
white turtleneck
gray mid-calf corduroy jumper
black opaque panty hose
black chunky-heeled suede loafers
red Bakelite bracelet

✿ **granny glasses**
red turtleneck
white overalls
white high-tops
red leather backpack

✿ **granny glasses**
bone silk shirt
tobacco suede wrap skirt
brown cowboy boots
string of amber beads

✿ **granny glasses**
white turtleneck
black flowered print skirt
black cowboy boots
black leather jacket

✿ **granny glasses**
kente print mid-calf slip dress
brown sandals
ivory earrings
amber bracelet
straw bag

h

A

B

C

E

F

HAIR CLIP

There are few accessories with as humble a beginning as the hair clip. Born as a tool for the stylist to section hair for color or cutting, women liked the tousled hair that the clip fortuitously created. Women frequently commented that sometimes they looked better while they were worked on than after they were done. It wasn't long before clips became a basic hair ornament.

Clips work equally well for every hair texture and volume. The best clips imported from France have a sturdy, dependable spring while inexpensive imports from Korea tend to break easily.

Clips can pile hair up on the head, pull it to one side, or capture a few side strands and leave the rest of the hair around the face. Both tortoiseshell and black plastic clips are the foundation of a clip collection. In pastel, bright colors, or decorated with rhinestones, clips make a more personal statement. Animal-print clips allow the wearer to take a few steps on the wild side.

HAT

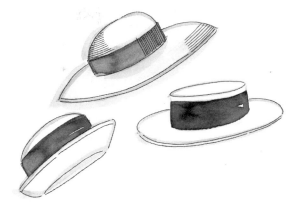

For centuries men wore hats as a visible symbol of occupation, nationality, politics, status, wealth, or religion. Women had a less complicated agenda—they just wanted to look good. Each fashion cycle has had its own unique style of hats which was worn by women of almost every age and rank. For example, at the turn of the century, the English boater was worn with equal enthusiasm by elegant Gibson girls, shy orphans, and saucy housemaids on their day off. When hat styles changed, last year's headgear was packed away without a second glance. Wearing an out-of-date hat was considered a major loss of fashion status.

Hats and hair have had a long and uneasy relationship. Some years hairstyles determined hat shape and size. A few decades later, hats were the fashion driver and hair had to follow their lead. For example, the tight small cloche needed—no, demanded—a short, flat

a glorious explosion in hat design and wear. Hat styles were frequently sparked by the Hollywood fashion designers. Manufacturers and hat designers watched in amazement as women passionately copied Garbo's slouch hat and dressed their children in Shirley Temple—style straw hats. They began to orchestrate hat/film promotions. Styles were featured in movie magazines and newsreels even before the actual movie was released. Some companies began lines with names like Cinema Fashions and Screen Star Styles, often with a label that featured the name or even the signature of the star who wore them.

Hats were not only a fashion statement, they were a grooming necessity. Before the days of the handheld hairdryer, women frequently struggled to maintain their hairstyles between weekly beauty parlor visits. The all-covering hat, worn all day between trips to the hairdresser, helped maintain the illusion of polished chic. The arrival of the personal hairdryer gave women the tool to style hair quickly at home. Hats took a distinct backseat as stylists such as Sassoon created easily maintained styles, so striking that hats seemed obstructive and redundant.

It took the beautiful Princess of Wales to nudge women back to thinking about hats. We will probably never go back to a fashion where women collected a wardrobe of hats to be worn day and

hairstyle. Once on the head, such hats all but destroyed a hairstyle, dictating that the hat be worn for the rest of the day. A few decades earlier the enormous piles of hair called for large hats that could perch on the big hair updo's of the Gibson girl.

From the 1920s to the '50s there was

night, indoors and out. We now use hats as a true accessory—to add emphasis, express personality, or finish a look.

Now that hats are a fashion option, rather than a requirement, there is no single style that dictates your choice. Instead, there are a range of hat styles that cover 200 years of men's and women's fashion history. The key to finding a flattering hat is persistence. Keep trying on different hat styles in different sizes and fabrics. When you look better with it than without it, the hat works for you. Each fall you will see berets (first worn by Roman legions) and derbys, a favorite of 19th-century Englishmen. In the summer, hat stands will be filled with boater hats, Panama hats, and white sailor hats. This variety offers you the opportunity to choose the shape and size that works best for your face and hair, rather than feeling pressured to wear the "hat of the moment."

The right hat provides finish and balance to an outfit. It can add curves to an angular face and interesting planes to a round one. What else but a hat keeps you warm, expresses personality, highlights your eyes, and makes you look taller?

(Also see ALPINE HAT, BERET, BASEBALL CAP, BOATER HAT, BRETON HAT, CARTWHEEL HAT, CLOCHE HAT, COWBOY HAT, DERBY, FEDORA, GARBO HAT, KNIT CAP, NEWSBOY CAP, PANAMA HAT, PILLBOX HAT, SAILOR HAT, STRAW HAT, TRILBY, TAM O' SHANTER.)

THE REAL MAD HATTER

The bizarre behavior characterized by the vase-shaped hat of the Mad Hatter in Lewis Carroll's "Alice in Wonderland" was derived from an actual 19th-century English workplace health problem. Exposed to felt dust saturated with mercury, hat workers became irritable, acted irrtionally, and shook with tremors. In the United States, the syndrome was known as the "Danbury Shakes," named after the Connecticut town famous for their hat manufacturing. Simply improving ventilation in the factories virtually eliminated the disease.

HEADBAND

The most famous headband is arguably the strip of black velvet worn by Alice on her journey through Wonderland. (In England headbands are still called Alice bands.) It remained an accessory for youths until Coco Chanel decided to soften the lines of her jersey knits and tailored jackets with the effortlessly feminine headband: it worked. The headband became the emblem of trim, girlish chic. When the headband came to the United States, the 1950s preppy took the concept literally and matched her headbands to the feminine pastel hues of the time. The headband lost its edge in the swirl of printed shirtwaists and embroidered linen bags, and was pushed to the back burner of style.

During the 1960s the hard headbands were upstaged by a wide, stretchy soft band. At least 2 inches thick and usually in black, this headband was the perfect accessory for the teased and fall-enhanced hairstyles that accompanied the "go-go" era. When the 1960s were finally over (it seemed like it lasted until the mid–1970s), the stretchy headband was rescued from the discarded pile of white vinyl boots and op art prints and adopted by runners. Now men and women gratefully strap on the stretchy band to absorb sweat as they pound out their daily miles.

To get the maximum impact from the classic headband refer to Chanel's original concept and use it to soften your most tailored pieces. For example, try a 2-inch black velvet headband with a white silk shirt and tailored gray wool pantsuit, or pair a navy grosgrain band (perhaps decorated with a flat bow) with a navy blazer, white T-shirt, and blue jeans.

When you try on headbands, think of them as hats with the power to flatter your face, not just something to keep your hair back. Experiment with different widths. As a general rule, broad faces are flattered by narrow headbands, thicker padded styles can halo a small face, while narrow bands with a side bow can add curves to a thin face.

How to Wear a Headband

✿ **black velvet headband**
  gray pantsuit
  white cashmere turtleneck sweater
  black Belgian loafers
  silver hoop earrings
  silver chain bracelet
  black nylon tote bag

✿ **navy grosgrain headband**
  navy pantsuit
  white cotton shirt
  white chunky socks
  navy suede loafers
  small gold hoop earrings
  navy satchel bag

❁ **narrow black velvet headband**
   black crew-neck sweater
   black collarless jacket
   black-and-royal-blue-checked
      wool skirt
   light black opaque panty hose
   black suede shoes
   gold and pearl earrings
   14– to 16–inch baroque
      pearl necklace

❁ **black velvet headband**
   black long cashmere
      turtleneck
   black mid-calf knit skirt
   black short granny boots
   small pearl stud earrings

❁ **Pucci print wide headband**
   turquoise short linen sheath
   hot pink cardigan tied
      over shoulders
   bright green thong sandals
   pearl stud earrings
   small yellow handbag

❁ **wide red plaid headband**
   white cotton T-shirt
   navy blazer
   straight-leg jeans
   white chunky socks
   tassel loafers
   small gold hoop earrings
   14-inch gold fine-link
      necklace
   navy satchel bag

❁ **cream braided headband**
   cream silk wrap blouse
   pink or banana yellow
      linen pantsuit
   pale-toned panty hose
   cream slingback pumps
   triple-strand pearl
      necklace
   pearl bracelet
   cream Chanel shoulder-strap bag

i

IVORY TIP SHEET

The Endangered Species Act of 1973 prohibited the importation of ivory from living elephants. Since it was impossible to judge if a piece was crafted from an elephant that died peacefully of old age or from one slaughtered for its tusks, craftsmen have turned to alternative substances. Tusks from whales, hippos, and even warthogs are used for ivory jewelry, but the most popular substitute is a vegetable ivory called Corzo. This football-sized nut grows on a palm tree found in South America. Corzo ivory is frequently used for buttons and beads. True African ivory can be distinguished from all other forms by the unique horizontal lines that texture the surface.

IVORY

There is something pure and primitive about ivory from the tusks of African and Indian elephants. Weighing up to 200 pounds, these creamy white tusks can be carved into beads, bracelets, and art objects.

You will find three basic styles of ivory jewelry. Ethnic designs from Africa, India, and Turkey feature large beads and chunky bracelets. African bracelets are often simply transverse sections of the actual tusk. Indian craftsmen frequently combine sections of ivory with hammered silver to create hinged bracelets. Pakistani jewelers often tint the ivory with a reddish pink dye, believing that such jewelry will lessen the pain of childbirth.

Pale white Oriental ivory earrings, pins, beads, and bracelets are decorated with delicate carved designs. Victorian pieces combined the native ivory with dainty traditional 19th-century designs. Jewelers bleached and polished the ivory, carving it into naturalistic leaves and flowers for bracelets, earrings, and pins.

Ivory is traditionally a warm-weather accessory. It seems to have a natural affinity with unpressed linens, raw silks, and nubby cottons. Ivory pieces blend easily with wood, shell, and turquoise jewelry. Delicate Victorian ivory pieces can be worn with a pale-colored tailored suit, as well as soft silk dresses.

How to Wear Ivory

❂ **ivory bead necklace**
pale yellow unpressed cotton shift
white espadrilles

❂ **ivory bangle bracelets**
off-white short-sleeved T-shirt
brown drawstring linen pants
alligator sandals
amber earrings
straw tote bag

❂ **three to four silver and ivory bangle bracelets**
black short-sleeved T-shirt
black linen pants
black suede ballet flats
small silver hoop earrings

❂ **ivory and silver bangle bracelets**
black long linen shift
black patent leather sandals or slides
silver earrings
silver bead necklace

❂ **multiple-strand ivory bead necklace**
❂ **mix of ivory and jade bangle bracelets**
olive green linen sleeveless top
olive green drawstring pants
bone mules

❂ **ivory earrings**
brown linen jumper
brown suede mules
silver cuff bracelet

j

J a d e

The carved flat jade discs that dangle in Chinese souvenir shops have been a symbol of heaven since Neolithic times. The most revered stone in China, jade is part of its national custom and religion. In a custom that began sixteen centuries before the birth of Christ, Chinese frequently hold a piece of jade in their hands when they have anything of importance to discuss.

The term "jade" is actually used for two different stones, creating confusion for both buyers and sellers. Jadeite, rare and highly desirable, was not used in China until after 1740. Nephrite, the old, true jade, is widely available and far less valuable. However, the carved jade pieces from centuries-old dynasties are considered national treasures and fabulously expensive. In other words, old jade is valued for its workmanship and history, whatever the type of stone. Contemporary pieces are judged more for the class of stone.

Jade varies in color from pale green (common) to imperial apple green (very rare) to dark spinach green (not uncommon). Frequently you will see inexpensive jade in tones of pink, amber, and lavender. Variations of color, brown veins, and light patches lower the value.

Jade jewelry is available in both carved and smooth beads, and flat discs, as well as rounded cabochon settings. The luminous stone looks beautiful with silks and pastels, but don't think that it works only with Far Eastern clothing styles. Jade mixes well with pearls and gold, adding both light and color. If you have ruddy skin tones, jade earrings will cool down the redness. If your skin has yellow undertones, wear jade away from the face in a ring or bracelet. If you frequently wear browns and greens, a jade bracelet can become one of your signature pieces.

H o w t o W e a r J a d e

✿ **pale green jade earrings**
✿ **jade bangle bracelet**
  bone linen skirt suit
  pale-toned panty hose
  bone and green Chanel pumps
  green, black, and white chiffon scarf
    tied as an ascot

✿ **18-inch strand of pale green jade beads**
  brown wool mid-calf dress
  brown ribbed tights
  brown suede clogs
  jade bangle bracelets

✿ **jade earrings**
✿ **onyx, jade, and pearl brooch**
  black fitted wool skirt suit
  black sheer panty hose
  black slingback pumps
  bottle-green suede envelope bag

✿ **jade pi** on silk cord
   deep green headband or hair clip
   oatmeal tweed turtleneck sweater
   brown mid-calf knit skirt
   brown cowboy boots
   amber bracelet

JADE SYMBOLS

You will see jade ornaments in a variety of shapes and images. Each one has a special meaning. When the Chinese give a present of jade, they choose a piece that mirrors their feelings.

- **Two men: friendship.**
- **Phoenix: good wishes for a young girl.**
- **Butterfly: good luck.**
- **Padlock: protects a child from danger.**
- **Bat on leaves: good fortune, happiness.**
- **String of jade beads: the king, strength, and power.**

JET

It was the death of Prince Albert that rocketed black jet stone to the most important jewelry material of the second half of the 19th century. When her beloved prince consort passed away in 1861, Queen Victoria began a period of mourning that was to last for more than 25 years. During this time she wore black mourning clothes and only black jewelry. The rest of England followed suit. . . and the little town of Whitby on the Yorkshire coast mined the jet from their cliffs and became the source of mourning jewelry for all of Europe.

Straight from the earth, Whitby jet is a brown–black substance formed by the effects of heat and pressure on ancient driftwood. It is extremely lightweight and can be cut and carved into extraordinary shapes. Frequently Victorian jewelers fashioned large pins or earrings with moveable or hanging parts. Every woman, whether or not she was in mourning, owned a selection of black jet pins, bracelets, and earrings.

The term "jet" is used interchangeably for similar black jewelry. Bog oak from the peat bogs of Ireland was a popular jet look-alike in the 1800s and was frequently shaped into shamrocks, harps, and other Celtic motifs by local craftsmen. French jet is actually black glass backed in lead. Somewhat less fragile, and definitely less costly, French jet

was molded into elaborate constructions of flowers, hearts, and stars, all connected by nearly invisible wires.

During the 1920s and '30s, jet was used in geometric art deco motifs. In the Southwest, American jet is called Apache tears and often was used in combination with turquoise and coral. Jet has a subtle, faceted shine that complements minimalist clothing. On its own, jet enlivens black, gray, and brown outfits, and a piece of jet jewelry is a striking accent on a pink Chanel-style suit with black trim.

How to Wear Jet

✿ **black jet earrings**
  white high-neck Victorian-style blouse
  black pleated pants
  white lace socks
  black velvet flats

✿ **wide black jet bracelet**
  black sleeveless linen shift
  black high-heeled
    alligator-patterned sandals
  diamond stud earrings

✿ **large black jet brooch**
  red wool jacket skirtsuit
  black sheer panty hose
  black pumps
  small gold hoop earrings
  gold bangle bracelet
  black envelope bag

✿ **multiple-strand black jet bead necklace**
  black short-sleeved silk sweater
  black linen pants
  black suede ballet flats
  tiny pearl earrings
  small black shoulder bag

✿ **black jet Victorian bracelet**
  red short linen dress
  black slingback shoes
  gold Victorian-style earrings

✿ **multiple-strand black jet necklace**
  black knit short
    crew-neck dress
  black opaque panty hose
  black high-heeled Mary Janes
  small gray pearl earrings

✿ **large black jet brooch**
  bright yellow or pink jacket
  black short skirt
  black sheer panty hose
  pearl earrings
  black Chanel bag

✿ **jet cuff bracelet**
  black velvet scrunchy or headband
  slim charcoal gray hip-length
    pull-over
  black stretch knit boot-cut pants
  black chunky high-heeled loafers
  small silver hoop earrings
  vintage 1960s black leather car coat

k

KELLY BAG

So named in the 1950s when Grace Kelly was often photographed carrying one, the Kelly is the ultimate status bag. Roomy, elegant, and pickpocket-proof, the Kelly bag was first introduced by Hermès in the late 1930s. The design was an adaptation of a much larger piece of luggage used to carry the riding tack of the European royals.

Hermès opened their doors in 1837, providing riding equipment to the most famous stables of France, czarist Russia, and England. When the automobile ended horse-drawn transportation in the late 1920s, Hermès branched out to handbags and luggage that incorporated equestrian motifs.

Authentic Kelly bags are expensive and hard to find. Hermès makes a limited number each year and frequently has a list of customers waiting to pay between two and ten thousand dollars for the privilege of owning an original Kelly. Copies of the Kelly range from beautiful to barely acceptable. Traditional colors of black, brown, and tan add classic accents, while pink, red, and yellow are irreverent and playful.

How to Wear a Kelly Bag

❁ **black Kelly bag** with black, white, and gray scarf tied to handle
   velvet headband or bow
   off-white sweater set
   charcoal gray pin-striped pants
   bone ribbed trouser socks
   black alligator loafers
   diamond stud earrings
   triple-strand pearl necklace

❁ **cranberry pigskin Kelly bag**
   cranberry turtleneck top
   brown tweed jacket
   taupe gabardine riding pants
   brown ankle-boots
   gold angel drop earrings

❁ **dark red large Kelly bag**
   black pantsuit
   white cotton blouse with French cuffs
   white ribbed trouser socks
   black leather platform oxfords
   diamond stud earrings
   ruby and rhinestone stud cuff links

❁ **black Kelly bag**
   off-white crepe 1940s-style blouse
      black vintage lambswool pearl
      decorated cardigan
   black gabardine pleated trousers
   black alligator belt
   black-and-white two-tone men's
      lace-up oxfords
   pearl stud earrings
   marcasite wristwatch

❁ **pink patent leather Kelly bag**
   white cotton polo shirt
   pink cotton sweater worn over the
      shoulders
   bright yellow-lime-and-pink-plaid
      slim cotton pants
   white ballet flats
   bright green plastic cat's-eye
      sunglasses
   pearl stud earrings

❁ **dark brown large alligator Kelly bag**
   navy V-necked cashmere sweater
   white straight-leg jeans
   dark brown cowboy ankle-boots
   pearl stud earrings
   brown, navy, gold, and cream silk ascot

❁ **bright orange Kelly bag**
   white cotton tank top
   vintage 1950s Hawaiian shirt in
      green, orange, yellow, and white
      print on a black ground
   black baggy linen trousers
   black linen mules
   brightly colored dangle earrings
      (palm tree and/or fish)
   black, orange, and green plastic
      bangle bracelets

KILTIE SHOES

Adapted from a Scottish golfing shoe, this sporty low-heeled style has a shawl or fringed tongue over the instep. For added support, better fit, and a touch of tradition, there is often a leather lace threaded around the side which ends in a tassel on the top of the fringe. Classic and casual, the kiltie works beautifully with wool pants and sweaters, as well as jeans and blazers. Kilties are a natural partner for all-season jeans, khakis, flannel, tweed, Scottish Highland sweaters and vests, and socks in argyle, Fair Isle, and paisley patterns.

How to Wear Kiltie Shoes

❁ **oxblood kiltie shoes**
camel cashmere polo sweater
brown tweed pants
brown and rust paisley wool socks
gold "shrimp" earrings
rust, gold, and hunter green
    silk print ascot

❁ **brown suede kiltie shoes**
gray cashmere turtleneck
gray flannel pants
brown leather belt
gray, brown, beige, and
    hunter green Fair Isle socks
amber stud earrings
tortoiseshell bracelets
brown Bugatti bag

❁ **black leather kiltie shoes**
black sweater set with gold buttons
mid-calf black-white-and-red-plaid
    kilt skirt
black opaque panty hose
small antique gold earrings
gold charm bracelet
black vintage men's long cashmere
    polo coat
red gloves
black nylon and red
    tartan backpack

❁ **brown leather kiltie shoes**
pink polo sweater
brown tweed riding jacket
white slim-leg jeans
brown and pink argyle socks
pearl stud earrings
brown nylon or suede backpack

KNIT CAP

The pull-on knit cap, worn for centuries by seamen, became part of the fashion mainstream when Ali MacGraw wore one in the 1969 movie *Goodbye Columbus.* According to the actress, they were filming silent bridge scenes on a winter day when it began to snow. She pulled on her favorite knit cap to continue filming and a new style was born. Along with mittens, mufflers, and snow boots, knit caps have remained a staple of winter. Fluffed with angora, airy in crochet, or trimmed with a cuff, this round, snug cap offers flattering warmth. Pull it down low over your forehead to emphasize your eyes.

How to Wear a Knit Cap

✿ **navy and cream snowflake knit cap**
white cable-knit sweater
blue jeans
green-flecked chunky wool socks
bluchers
navy peacoat
green gloves
green-and-navy-plaid backpack

✿ **brown flecked knit cap**
white turtleneck
brown corduroy overalls
brown, orange, and cream socks
brown hiking boots with orange laces
loden duffel coat
brown polar fleece mittens

✿ **black angora knit cap**
gray wool knit mid-calf dress
black leather granny boots
small marcasite and jet earrings
silver cuff bracelet
black velvet backpack

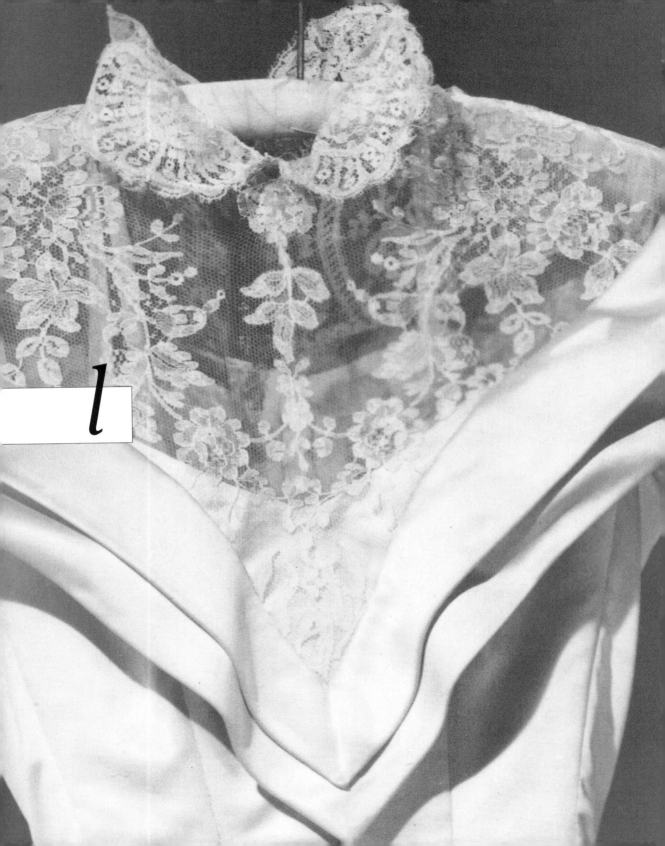

l

LACE

Depending on how and where it is worn, lace can be seductive and erotic or young and innocent. For example, a touch of lace, perhaps with a cameo or pearls, immediately softens a severe black suit. On the other hand a pair of black lace stockings have the opposite effect with a short black dress, cranking up the sexiness.

There are two basic forms: bobbin lace (such as Antwerp and Chantilly) is created by the manipulation of many threads and is usually worked on a pillow. Needlepoint lace (such as alençon and Venetian) is created by looping yarn or thread through a single needle to stitch an elaborate pattern on a fixed base. Prior to World War I lace was as popular as buttons as a clothing ornament. In the 1970s, lace was used as a true accessory as lace handkerchiefs, collars, gloves, and cobwebby knitted scarves to soften the edge of masculine tweeds and men's tailored looks of the *Annie Hall* era. Touches of lace seemed to represent security as we moved from traditional women's roles to the new dynamics of the "liberated" woman.

Choose lace boldly and take advantage of its chameleonlike ability to change attitudes. Black lace socks peeking from below a pair of black pants paired with a white linen shirt turns a classic look seductive. Exchanging these for a pair of white lace socks and black ballet flats adds girlish, gentle notes.

How to Wear Lace

❃ **narrow piece of off-white lace** wound around neck and tucked into collar
brown cashmere crew-neck sweater
bone flannel pants
brown loafers or low-heeled pumps
coral and pearl earrings
brown shoulder bag

❁ **black point d'esprit lace panty hose**
  black satin bow barrette with black
    crocheted snood
  black short velvet tank dress
  black silk high-heeled sandals
  rhinestone stud earrings

❁ **lacy trouser socks**
  cream cashmere crew-neck sweater
  brown wool pleated trousers
  brown alligator belt
  brown alligator-patterned loafers
  pearl stud earrings
  gold chain bracelets

❁ **stole of antique lace**
  brown short shift
  cream-and-brown two-tone slingback
    pumps
  gold and pearl drop earrings
  brown and cream vintage beaded bag

❁ **black lace panty hose**
  black velvet pantsuit
  white satin blouse
  black high-heeled satin pumps
  antique gold earrings
  gold and pearl antique
    Victorian bracelet

❁ **cream oblong lace scarf**
  hair pinned up with ivory hair clip
  baby blue mid-calf slip dress with
    lace trim
  cream low-heeled sandals
  delicate pearl and gold drop earrings

❁ **lace handkerchief**
  arranged in pocket
  cream sweater
  brown tweed blazer
  gray flannel trousers
  brown paisley socks
  brown suede loafers
  pearl earrings
  garnet and gold bracelet

❁ **off-white oblong lace scarf**
  bone gabardine pantsuit
  bone sheer trouser socks
  bone and black Chanel-style
    flats or pumps
  gold earrings
  chunky gold chain bracelet
  black patent leather shoulder bag

❁ **white lace camisole**
  red cashmere V-necked sweater
  blue jeans
  white platform sneakers
  pearl stud earrings

LOAFERS

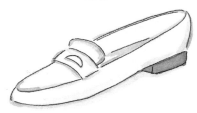

The first truly chic casual shoe, this low-
heeled slip-on originated in Norway. In
1936, a Maine shoemaker by the name of

Harry Bass negotiated with a Scandinavian manufacturer to refine their shoe for American tastes. He named them "Weejuns" after the two final syllables of Norwegian. They were introduced into fashion by European trendsetters and social leaders on the Riviera, where they were worn both for comfort and a badge of sophistication. By the late 1950s Weejuns (or loafers, as they were often called) were firmly established as *the* collegiate status symbol.

In addition to the traditional "penny" loafer, three popular variations were introduced over the last fifty years: driving shoes, Gucci, and Belgian. Driving shoes, created by J.P. Tod, were designed with rubber nubs across the sole and heel, a feature designed to help a race car driver grip the accelerator pedal. These rubber bumps also absorb impact, making this type of loafer a lightweight, soft, and comfortable walking shoe. They have become the favorite footwear of Fiat chairman Gianni Agnelli, who even wears a patent leather version with dinner jackets.

Gucci loafers, introduced in the late 1930s, maintain the same basic loafer style but use a softer leather and decorate the instep with a goldtone snaffle bit.

Belgian loafers, originated by the Henri Bendel store in the 1940s, feature a high vamp decorated with a small flat bow. In addition to plain leather, Belgian loafers are frequently made in solid and patterned suedes and velvets. True Belgian loafers are completely handmade to order. The shoe is delivered with a soft sole, and the new

owner wears it indoors for a few weeks until it conforms to the foot. Finally, a hard sole is added to complete a perfect fit. This loafer was too stylish to stay exclusive, and can be found ready-made in better shoe departments.

The loafer continues to be reinvented: from the original brown leather style to the tasseled version; from the lug-soled workboot style to the riotous colors of royal blue, turquoise, hot pink, red, and green; and from patent leather to leopard prints.

How to Wear Loafers

❂ **black velvet Belgian loafers**
   white silk turtleneck
   black velvet bolero jacket
   red plaid tartan wool slim-leg pants
   red plaid trouser socks
   square onyx and gold earrings

❂ **brown suede loafers**
   gray cashmere crew-neck sweater
   brown glen plaid pleated trousers
   brown suede belt
   gray cashmere socks
   small gold earrings
   honey-amber choker
   tortoiseshell cuff bracelet
   brown leather backpack

❂ **black suede loafers**
   black velvet bow barrette
   red turtleneck sweater
   gray flannel trousers
   black faux alligator belt
   gray, red, and black Fair Isle socks
   red Kelly bag

❂ **oxblood loafers**
   white T-shirt
   navy lightweight wool cropped
      bomber jacket
   khaki slim-leg pants
   diamond stud earrings
   paisley vintage men's dress scarf
   diamond tennis bracelet

❂ **white leather driving shoes** worn
      without socks
   white cotton shirt
   yellow cotton sweater worn over
      the shoulders
   white linen pants
   white leather belt
   tank wristwatch
   turquoise leather Kelly bag with
      Pucci-print scarf tied to handle

❂ **leopard and black leather loafers**
   black cashmere turtleneck sweater
   black cashmere cardigan worn over
      the shoulders
   black wool hip-stitched short skirt
   black opaque tights
   smooth polished gold clip earrings
   small black suede tote bag

LOCKET

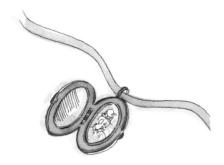

There is something intensely personal and secretive about lockets. Dangling from a charm bracelet or hanging on a chain around the neck, lockets are the most sentimental of accessories. They first appeared around the time of Henry VII, but it wasn't until the romantic Victorian period that they became a fashion necessity. Round, oval, square, or heart-shaped, they carried small photographs of or locks of hair from special loved ones.

Lockets have been mass-produced for decades and can be found in jewelry stores and flea markets. Traditionally lockets have been a "sweetheart" gift from an admirer or loving relative. Today it is a wonderful present to give yourself, placing inside a small snapshot of a friend, lover, or child.

When wearing a locket, be aware of size and proportion. A smaller locket works best on a thin, short chain. A larger locket looks wonderful on longer chains that hold the locket midway between your waist and the bottom of your bust line. Vintage gold and brass lockets are perfect for traditional feminine styles while sleek silver and gold lockets enhance trendier silhouettes.

❂ **medium-length gold oval locket**
cream silk notched-collar shirt
navy blazer
blue jeans
brown alligator loafers
diamond stud earrings
brown leather backpack

❂ **small gold locket on 14-inch gold chain**
short-sleeved white T-shirt
pink and white print slip dress
white quilted Chanel-style flats
small pearl drop earrings
straw bag

✿ **gold charm bracelet with lockets and hearts**
mid-calf black linen shift
black Chanel-style flats
small gold Victorian-style earrings

LUCITE

When you start off life as a material for industrial shelving, the transition to fashion accessory is bound to be a little rocky. As a contemporary of Bakelite, Lucite was a distant second choice for plastic jewelry. Clear, cold, and angular, Lucite could not compete with the rich, luminous colors and curves of Bakelite. During the 1920s and '30s, Lucite was often seen in clear flat pins and earrings with a small flower embedded in the center. In the late 1950s, Lucite had the dubious honor of becoming the material of choice for the elaborately decorated plastic handbags that became the emblem of Miami chic.

It took nothing less than an international fascination with the prospect of space travel to establish Lucite as a legitimate accessory material. The race to land a man on the moon inspired designers to create a new high-tech aesthetic. The Lucite earring became the perfect accompaniment to the short geometric Sassoon haircut, and a Lucite ring was the only accessory needed with a futuristic Courreges jumpsuit.

Lucite still works beautifully with monochromatic minimalist silhouettes. Keep an eye out for '60s Lucite jewelry in flea markets, thrift shops, and tag sales.

✿ **Lucite cuff bracelet**
black wool turtleneck sweater
slim black wool pants
black-and-white polka-dot socks
black suede loafers
diamond stud earrings

✿ **chunky Lucite ring**
gray gabardine pantsuit
white T-shirt
black cowboy boots
diamond stud earrings
black backpack

✿ **short strand of large Lucite beads**
mid-calf black linen shift
black platform sandals
black and white Bakelite bracelet
black straw tote bag

✿ **vintage Lucite handbag**
black pantsuit
white T-shirt
short white socks
black suede platform sandals
vintage black jacket

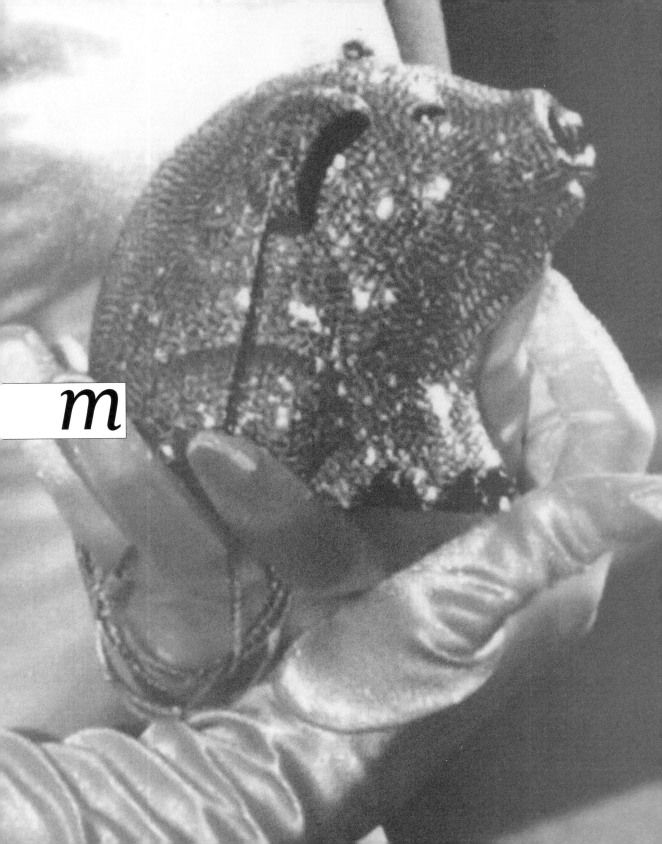

m

MARCASITE

Marcasite has been adding light and movement since the time of the ancient Greeks. Set in silver or pewter, marcasite gets its sparkle by refracting light, rather than from internal light found in true diamonds.

Marcasite stones, which are actually a form of crystallized iron, are used, pavé style, in pins, earrings, bracelets, and pendants. The best pieces are constructed from individual stones, while the less expensive items are made from machine-made strips.

Marcasite jewelry was as correct in the 1920s and '30s as a pair of gold earrings are today. You can still find many wonderful examples with art deco motifs in flea markets and antique shops. For impact, choose good-sized pieces with strong, clear shapes like rectangles, hearts, bows, and circles. Small pieces may look cute on black velvet trays, but tend to get lost on modern clothing. If you have a collection of small pins, group them together for better impact. Marcasites look great against black or gray and add a sparkle to sweaters, coats, and jackets. To avoid looking like a store display, blend marcasite with silver or diamond jewelry, rather than wearing a complete set of earrings, pins, and necklace. The soft glow of silver and the hot sparkle of diamonds will bring out the light and shape of a well-chosen piece of marcasite.

How to Wear Marcasite

✿ **marcasite bracelet**
   black sweater set
   black pants
   black ballet flats
   diamond stud earrings

✿ **large marcasite pin**
   worn on shoulder
   black boots
   black coat

✿ **marcasite art deco pin**
   worn on shoulder
   white cuffed shirt
   black jacket
   black pants
   black suede loafers
   black Bugatti bag

✿ **marcasite earrings**
✿ **mix of silver and marcasite bangle bracelets**
   black linen shift
   black platform slides
   black straw bag

✿ black cashmere scarf knotted
   around neck and anchored
   with **marcasite pin**
   gray sweater set
   gray flannel trousers
   black suede loafers
   diamond stud earrings

❀ **wide marcasite cuff bracelet**
  black short-sleeved T-shirt
  black linen pants
  black mules
  small silver hoop earrings

❀ **marcasite heart pendant**
  gray or black velvet shirt
  black wool pants
  black suede Chanel flats

❀ **marcasite pin worn** on shoulder
  gray flannel pantsuit
  black ankle-boots
  black Kelly bag

❀ **cluster of three to four small**
  marcasite pins worn on the shoulder
  gray sweater set
  gray or black pants
  suede Belgian loafers

MARY JANES

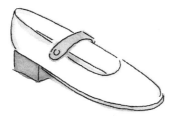

A classic. Originally worn by children, this patent leather slipper features a rounded toe and an instep strap that buckles on the side. Popular since the early 19th century, they were named Mary Janes after a character in the Buster Brown comic strip. Modern adult versions come in a variety of heel heights that range from $1/2$ inch to 3 inches and in a rainbow of colors. The open space from the toe to the strap offers possibilities to show off interesting patterns or unexpected solid colors. Mary Janes add innocence to a plain black dress, whimsy to a long print skirt, and insouciance to a tailored pantsuit. Platform Mary Janes add a note of humor to everything.

How to Wear Mary Janes

❀ **black suede Mary Janes**
  with 2-inch heels
  white mock turtleneck top
  black vintage wool suit jacket
  black and white rayon miniskirt
  black opaque panty hose
  vintage pearl earrings
  chunky pearl cuff bracelet

❀ **brown leather Mary Janes**
  with 3-inch heels
  short brown short-sleeved
    sweater dress
  brown opaque tights
  chunky short amber necklace
  wide tortoiseshell cuff bracelet

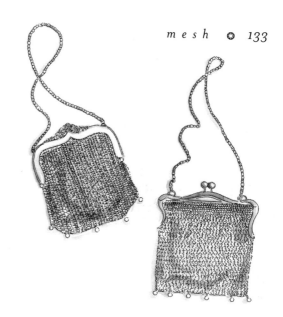

✿ **bone leather high-heeled Mary Janes**
taupe Breton hat with ribbon around the crown
pink linen skirt suit
bone sheer panty hose
small pearl stud earrings
taupe or faux crocodile envelope bag

✿ **black high-heeled Mary Janes**
black turtleneck
charcoal short wool skirt
black tights
chunky silver hoop earrings
chunky silver bead necklace
black Bugatti bag

✿ **navy high-heeled Mary Janes**
navy linen fitted pantsuit with cream buttons
cream linen shell
bone ribbed trouser socks
chunky gold earrings
thick gold chain bracelet

MESH

This fabric, woven from metallic threads, was originally worn by knights in the Middle Ages, but is now used in women's accessories—primarily for belts and small handbags. Around the waist or on a long chain hanging like a pendant around the neck, a mesh bag in gold or silver tones adds a soft, gentle sparkle.

Mesh belts may look stiff and unyielding, but they are surprisingly pliable on the body. In the 19th century mesh bags were considered appropriate for any occasion. More recently they are usually worn with cocktail and evening clothes for a touch of individuality and nostalgia.

How to Wear Mesh

✿ **narrow silver mesh belt**
gray crew-neck long-sleeved sweater
dark gray gabardine pleated trousers
dark gray men's dress socks
black textured leather loafers
small silver and marcasite earrings
wristwatch with black lizard wristband

✿ **gold mesh drawstring bag**
black velvet strapless evening dress
black high-heeled satin sandals
black and gold drop earrings
gold and pearl cuff bracelet

✿ **multicolored vintage mesh bag**
  yellow linen pantsuit
  white Chanel pumps with gold toes
  small antique earrings

✿ **silver mesh belt** worn at the hip
  black ankle-length jersey T-shirt dress
  black platform mules
  silver tassel drop earrings
  sculpted silver cuff bracelet

✿ **silver mesh "kerchief"**
  fill-in necklace
  gray flannel pantsuit
  white silk blouse
  gray opaque panty hose
  gray satin sandals
  silver and pearl earrings
  at least 4 inches of silver bangle
    bracelets
  gray kid envelope bag with
    silver and marcasite closure

✿ **gold mesh belt**
  white tank top
  white silk blazer
  white silk pants
  white kid mules
  small gold hoop earrings
  pearl necklace
  tiny gold ankle bracelet

✿ **antique mesh purse**
  mid-calf flowered georgette slip dress
  bone sandals
  Chinese jade "pi" earrings

COLLECTING MESH BAGS

Many of the mesh bags sold today are vintage, made between 1900 and 1940. The most desirable examples were manufactured by Whiting and Davis. Prior to 1924, mesh bags were constructed by hand, a labor-intensive and costly endeavor. George Whiting developed a process that produced mesh on a machine, making the bags affordable to all women. The best bags were formed of sterling or silver plate. One of the most popular designs was the Princess Mary with the famous fold-over closure. Available in large and small styles, the graceful purse promised not to interfere with dancing.

MINAUDIÈRE

The minaudière is an elegant hard-sided evening bag created by Van Cleef and Arpels in 1930 when Charles Arpels noticed that one of his clients was using a metal Lucky Strike cigarette box as a purse. He adapted the look and named it after the wife of his partner, Estelle Van Cleef, who was minaudière (charming). At first minaudières were made of

How to Wear a Minaudière

❂ **Mickey Mouse minaudière**
  black velvet pantsuit
  white men's tailored blouse
  white thin socks
  black satin high-heeled sandals
  rhinestone stud earrings
  bright silk Mickey Mouse necktie

❂ **black beaded minaudière**
  black mock turtleneck
  black vintage fitted wool jacket with
    beading
  black gabardine pants
  black ankle-boots
  diamond stud earrings

precious metals and jewels, but the look was too delicious to remain exclusive. Within a decade you could find the dainty purse on female arms throughout America.

The charm and workmanship of the minaudière provides a shot of color and light to a plain suit or shift. Look for vintage mother-of-pearl, petit point, or beaded minaudières in flea markets and antique stores. Try changing the short wrist strap for a long chain that crosses the chest or hangs the small bag from your shoulder or neck.

THE PLAYFUL PURSE

The contemporary minaudière of Judith Leiber is arguably the most impressive evening bag in any room it enters. Beautifully decorated with up to 10,000 individually applied rhinestones, the amusing shapes seem to nestle happily in your hand. Placed on the table during dinner, it is far more like portable art than a mere purse. In recent years the most popular shapes include Mickey Mouse, a red heart, and a little pink pig.

✿ needlepoint minaudière
with long chain
brown long shift
brown sandals
garnet drop earrings

✿ vintage mother-of-pearl minaudière
rose linen mid-calf slip dress
bone ballet flats
small pearl stud earrings

✿ happy-face minaudière
yellow charmeuse jewel-neck
    back-buttoned blouse
red cashmere cardigan
black velvet pants
yellow socks
black patent leather tuxedo pumps
bright red lipstick

MITTENS

 Worn for centuries to keep warm, mittens became a fashion statement in the 1920s at Saint Moritz and Innsbruck, the winter playgrounds of the rich and royal. The introduction of international skiing and skating competitions inspired the development of decorative hand-knit mittens for both competitors and spectators. The local artisans used traditional Scandinavian designs to replace dull gray and brown wool mittens. Casual, warm, and colorful, mittens became a wonderful splash of color and style on a cold winter day. Mittens can be warmer than gloves because the hand creates its own body heat. You can find mittens in traditional Nordic patterns such as snowflakes and reindeer, Fair Isle knits, and cable wool patterns, as well as rugged shearling-lined suede.

How to Wear Mittens

✿ red and black Scandinavian
pattern mittens
red beret
white roll-neck sweater
black mid-calf wool skirt
red wool chunky socks
black ankle-boots
black and white vintage men's
    tweed coat

✿ red, cream, and brown
Fair Isle wool mittens
red chunky cable-knit pullover
taupe riding jodhpurs
brown desert boots
tan shearling-lined coat
cognac leather shoulder bag

✿ **green-and-navy-plaid mittens**
　　white, blue, and green knit cap
　　white turtleneck
　　green-and-navy-plaid flannel shirt
　　blue jeans
　　brown hiking boots
　　hunter green peacoat

✿ **black and white patterned mittens**
　　yellow hip-length pullover
　　black stretch pants
　　black ankle-boots
　　black quilted down vest

✿ **white ski mittens**
　　navy knit cap with pom-pom
　　white fishermen's knit sweater
　　hunter green corduroy overalls
　　white snow boots
　　white fishermen's knit muffler
　　hot pink quilted waist-length
　　　sleeveless parka

MOCCASINS

Soft-soled shoes, made and worn by Native Americans, moccasins are distinctively decorated with bead embroi-dery or fringe. These comfortable, casual shoes are usually found in luggage brown and white. In red leather, they add color and quick energy to dressed-down clothes. Moccasins are an indoor shoe for the winter and an outdoor shoe for the summer. Despite their rugged attitude, the soft soles make them some-what fragile. If you wear them in the rain, expect to get wet.

How to Wear Moccasins

✿ **white moccasins**
　　white T-shirt
　　white jeans
　　turquoise socks
　　small silver hoop earrings
　　silver and turquoise cuff bracelet

✿ **red moccasins**
　　white cotton shirt
　　blue jeans
　　brown leather cowboy belt
　　red bandanna neckerchief
　　pearl stud earrings
　　brown leather backpack

✿ **luggage brown moccasins**
　　white T-shirt
　　hunter green small-cable-knit
　　　cardigan
　　brown corduroy pants
　　yellow cashmere socks
　　gold earrings
　　yellow muffler

✿ **luggage brown moccasins**
  blue-and-white-striped shirt
  khaki slim-leg pants
  luggage brown belt
  white chunky socks
  small gold hoop earrings
  gold chain bracelets

MULES

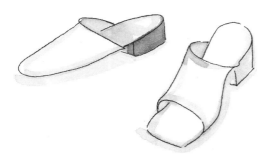

These shoes have attitude. Backless with heels that range from chunky flats to tall stilettos, mules are clearly not designed for hard work or fast walking. They are insolent shoes, openly declaring that you will not be rushed. Period.

In the 1970s Olivia Newton-John caused a sensation in the movie *Grease* with her makeover from good girl to biker babe. The red Charles Jourdan mules she wore the in the last scene electrified not only 8-year-old girls and boys, but the fashion trendies in Saint-Tropez.

By definition mules are backless shoes with a closed toe, while slides are backless and open-toed. However, the two terms are used interchangeably to describe all varieties of backless footwear.

For all their studied languor, mules can be challenging to fit. By design the shoe is held on the foot by the single strip of material across the instep. This strap needs to be tight enough to secure the shoe on the foot, yet loose enough to allow the foot to slip into the shoe until the top of the toes touch the tip of the sole. Keep trying on different styles and shapes until they feel delicious.

How to Wear Mules

✿ **black chunky leather mules with 2- to 3-inch heels**
  black turtleneck sweater
  gray flannel miniskirt
  silver chain belt
  black opaque panty hose
  silver earrings

✿ **navy satin high-heeled slides**
  navy velvet ankle-length dress
  navy semi-sheer panty hose
  diamond stud earrings
  vintage mesh or beaded bag

✿ **bone mules**
  pastel watercolor print long slip dress
  pearl stud earrings
  straw tote bag

❂ **silver slides with black soles and heels**
white cotton men's-tailored
   shirt with French cuffs
black cigarette pants
black alligator belt
onyx stud earrings with silver trim
men's onyx cuff links

❂ **turquoise linen slides**
black T-shirt
black linen pants
turquoise and silver earrings
2 to 3 silver chain necklaces
silver bracelet with large turquoise
   stone
black nylon tote bag

❂ **pale blue leather slides**
multicolored pastel flowered slip dress
pale yellow cotton crew-neck worn
   over the shoulders
aquamarine stud earrings
double-strand fine gold chain ankle
   bracelet
big straw tote bag

❂ **white slides with brown heels**
African print headwrap
white tank-top T-shirt
banana yellow linen shirt worn
   as a jacket
matching African print
   ankle-length skirt
straw tote bag

❂ **black satin open-toe high-heeled slides**
black satin hair bow on low ponytail
black crepe tank dress
turquoise cashmere cardigan tied
   around shoulders
diamond stud earrings
turquoise Chinese satin
   brocade tote bag

❂ **brown leather low-heeled slides**
white Panama hat
white lace camisole
cotton button-down shirt
white cotton slim-leg pants
braided leather belt
wide straw tote bag with
   tortoiseshell handle
pearl stud earrings

❂ **blue-and-white gingham mules**
blue plaid scrunchy
white cotton short-sleeved shirt
blue and white varsity sweater
white capri pants
small pearl drop earrings

❂ **brown leather low-heeled slides**
white sleeveless button-down
   shirt
khaki slim-leg pants
brown braided belt
pearl stud earrings
natural straw tote bag

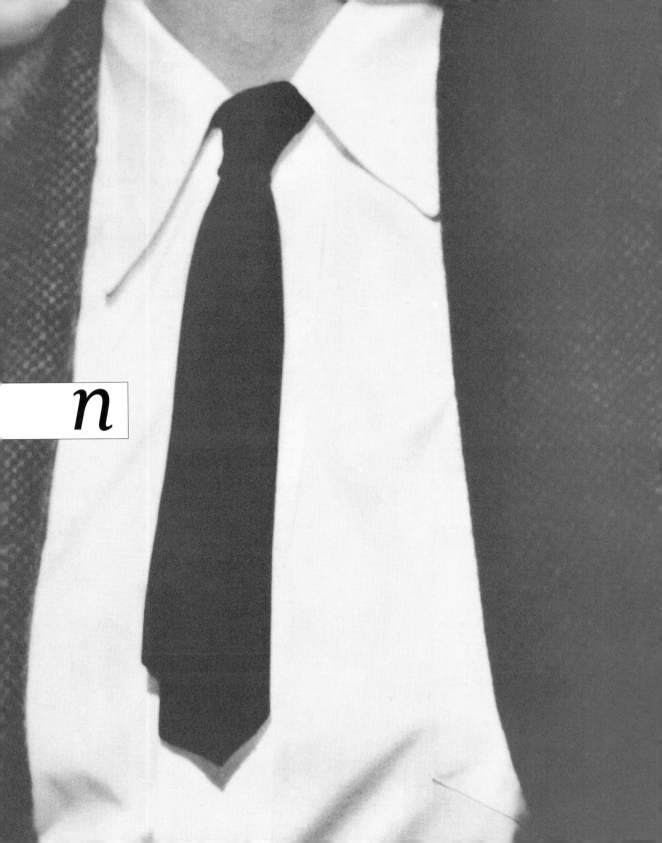

n

NATIVE AMERICAN JEWELRY

Native Americans of the Southwest have worn turquoise and shell jewelry throughout their history. "Traditional" Native American jewelry began in the 1870s as a seamless blend of European metalwork techniques and Indian culture. At first, the earliest silver work was added to ancient ceremonies as symbols of power and wealth, but soon silver was adopted for personal wear. Some of the designs, such as the bear claw, were derived from Indian legends, while others, such as the crescent-shaped *naja*, were adopted from Spanish motifs.

During hard times Native Americans would take some of their jewelry to the trading post and pawn it for credit. They proved to be so popular that traders hired Native craftsmen to create new pieces of jewelry to sell in their stores. To encourage production, they provided the self-taught artisans with silver, turquoise, and coral for their designs. In the 1880s Fred Harvey commissioned the first large-scale order of Native American jewelry to be sold at his Harvey House restaurants along the Acheson Topeka and Santa Fe Railroad. (Remember Judy Garland in *The Harvey Girls*? It's the same Harvey.) As a train pulled into a station, Native Americans would greet the passengers with baskets of silver and turquoise jewelry for sale.

Originally the pieces varied little from region to region. Over time, though, distinct tribal styles began to develop. Navajo was distinguished by heavy, often irregularly shaped pieces of turquoise, and massive, rather than dainty, silver work. They were famous for their silver concha belt and squash blossom necklace. Zuni developed the needlepoint setting using small pear-shaped pieces of turquoise set in clusters of silver. They also revived two ancient jewelry forms— hand-rolled beads of turquoise and fetishlike animals worn around the neck. The fetish is a natural or carved rock in which a spirit is thought to dwell. If the fetish is well treated, it will protect the wearer. The pueblo dwellers of San Domingo made similar types of fetish jewelry. Hopi styles, which were developed in the 1930s, used an all-silver overlay technique. Traditional Native American symbols such as the bear claw and feather were etched and darkened into the silver and formed into bracelets, rings, and earrings.

Collectors divide Native American jewelry into three time periods. The earliest pieces, made between 1850 and 1900, are extremely rare and start at $10,000 for a small buckle. They were quite simple in design with tiny irregularities in the metal from rough hand tools. Jewelry made between 1900 and 1950 is considered the classic period of design. These buckles, pins, bracelets, belts, necklaces, and earrings follow traditional tribal designs. They are still made today, but contemporary artists have expanded the concepts of Southwestern jewelry into more modern forms. Many of these designers sign

their work and have established an enthusiastic following.

The value of Native American jewelry depends on the weight of the silver, quality of the stones, workmanship, and, if applicable, the age of the piece, but you should select pieces that you will want to wear and not just view them as an investment.

In western states both men and women wear Native American jewelry on a daily basis. Under the bright sunlight and a palate of colors from a painted desert, the jewelry looks right on practically every occasion. Against a cityscape of gray steel and glass, masses of silver and turquoise jewelry can look less appropriate. Think about combining a single piece of Southwestern jewelry with other modern silver jewelry. For example, if you are lucky enough to own a Navajo silver concha belt, wrap it over a mid-calf-length black skirt and turtleneck sweater and pair it with a 2-inch silver cuff bracelet and small silver hoop earrings. Wear the same earrings with three to four thin silver and turquoise bracelets, a white cotton shirt, blue jeans, and a pair of white slip-on Keds.

There are several ways to collect Native American jewelry. Some people concentrate on a single tribe, while others acquire various tribal styles. Often a woman will buy just one spectacular piece, wear it with everything, and make it her fashion signature.

How to Wear Native American Jewelry

✿ **3-inch heavy Navajo cuff bracelet**
black turtleneck
black wool pants
black suede loafers
silver teardrop earrings

✿ **silver concha belt**
white linen shirt
black mid-calf suede skirt
black boots
silver button earrings

✿ **silver squash blossom necklace**
white turtleneck
black mid-calf knit or velvet jumper
black tights
black cowboy boots

✿ **silver concha pin** on jacket
blue denim shirt
short black wool jacket
black slim pants
black ankle-boots
small silver hoop earrings
black suede backpack

✿ **four to five thin silver and turquoise bracelets**
black short-sleeved mock turtleneck
black linen pants
black suede flats
silver button earrings

✿ **four or five thin silver and turquoise bracelets**
black crew-neck sweater
black wool pants
black cowboy boots
silver hoop earrings

✿ **triple strands of Pueblo fetish beads** wrapped around the neck
cranberry crushed velvet peasant dress
black boots
small turquoise earrings

✿ **16-inch strand of rough turquoise beads**
off-white linen blouse
brown short suede wrap skirt
brown alligator-patterned sandals
ivory earrings

✿ **large turquoise and silver cuff bracelets,** one worn on each arm
white mid-calf linen dress
white sandals
silver stud earrings

✿ **silver bird-in-flight brooch** pinned at neck
✿ **turquoise and silver sculpted cuff bracelet**
gray oversized cotton shirt worn untucked
brown bias-cut tweed long skirt
black tooled leather belt
white pushed-down socks
black suede ballet flats
turquoise-framed eyeglasses

NECKLACE

The urge to adorn the neck seems to be inborn and fundamental. Cavemen hung strings of shells and nuts around their necks even before they figured out how to stitch animal skins into clothing. Toddlers everywhere instinctively drape beads and ribbons around their necks, peering in the mirror to admire the effect. Kings wore the necklace to signify power, while priests used them to perform religious ceremonies.

Today it is hard to think of an occasion where a necklace would be inappropriate. A thin gold chain that hugs the throat adds a welcome flash of light to a bathing suit or plain white T-shirt; a pearl necklace brings a glow to tailored silks and tweeds; a multiple-strand choker of crystal beads changes a plain black sweater into an interesting statement; a long strand of shells is the perfect finish to an unpressed linen tank dress.

The necklace can be classified by length and form. The shortest necklace, 12–16 inches, nestles at the base of the neck. This length is frequently used for thin gold chains, pearls, and chunky multiple strands of beads. Victorian and Edwardian jewelers frequently made coral, amber, or pearl swag necklaces in this dainty length.

If you have a short or somewhat thick neck, a better choice might be the 16- to 24-inch necklace. Designed to fall at least 12 inches below your chin, this length works well for pearls, shells, and beads of semiprecious materials (such as amber, ivory, jade, and amethyst), as well as gold chains with and without lockets. This length works well if a large bust doesn't get in the way.

The matinee length, at 30–35 inches, should end at the waist area and is perfect worn alone or as the carrier for a pendant or watch.

The opera length, a 48- to 128-inch strand, originated in the 1890s in the form of a string of pearls to wear to the opera or other formal occasions. Usually worn wrapped twice around the neck, they are elegant and slimming for women over 5 feet 2 inches.

Most of us own a wide range of necklace styles and lengths, but usually wear the same ones over and over. To evaluate your necklace collection, divide your strands into two piles. On one side put the pieces that you wear frequently; keep the pieces that tend to stay at home in another pile. Look for similarities in each group. Are they related in length, style, and material? For example, if you favor tailored elegant clothing, the most popular style will probably be gold chains and pearls, while the least-worn group may include a turquoise pendant or a strand of cowrie shells. Thumb through this book to find ways to wear your "orphan" necklaces.

How to Wear a Necklace

⚙ **short thin gold chain**
  white cotton shirt with rolled-up
    sleeves
  blue jeans
  brown driving shoes
  pearl stud earrings
  brown backpack

⚙ **16-inch amber necklace**
  cream crew-neck sweater
  taupe jacket
  gray pants
  brown alligator loafers
  tiny antique gold earrings
  brown Bugatti bag

❁ **triple-strand pearl choker**
black strapless velvet gown
black satin shoes
pearl and diamond earrings
black satin bag

❁ **multiple-strand chunky crystal necklace**
charcoal gray short-sleeved cashmere
dress
black semi-opaque panty hose
black suede high-heeled loafers
antique jet earrings

❁ **16-inch strand of carved ivory beads**
pale yellow unpressed shift
bone mules
ivory earrings
straw bag

❁ **24-inch gold chain**
navy suit
bone notched-collar silk shirt
navy slingback pumps
pearl and gold earrings
antique gold bracelets

❁ **30-inch silver chain with heart pendant**
black turtleneck
black pants
black suede loafers
silver hoop earrings
silver cuff bracelet

NECKTIE

The necktie has always been a purely decorative piece of clothing. Despite its lack of function, it has been one of the enduring masculine symbols, and when worn by a woman sends a powerful yet often ambiguous message. For example, Marlene Dietrich used a men's tie with classic men's suits and coats along with her trilby hat and ladylike gloves. She created an androgynous but seductive image that fascinates to this day. By contrast, Diane Keaton in the movie *Annie Hall* used a wide loosely knotted tie to create an original, sweetly goofy image.

The beautiful colors and patterns of

WHO INVENTED THE NECKTIE?

The fashion tie is usually attributed to the French, but it turns out that they got the original concept from a regiment of 17th-century Croatian mercenaries. Frenchmen adapted the muslin and linen scarves that the foreign soldiers wrapped around their necks, naming them cravats (French for Croats). The concept quickly spread to England and has remained a fashion essential for more than three centuries.

both contemporary and vintage ties add a shot of bright movement to sportswear. They can be threaded through belt loops for a sash, tied with a low loose knot around the neck, or in bright satin can be worn with a tux for evening.

How to Wear a Necktie

✿ red, blue, and yellow regimental tie
white crisp cotton shirt
blue and white seersucker pants
white bucks
chunky white socks
small gold hoop earrings
gold chain-link bracelets
yellow and white tote bag

✿ cranberry-and-brown-toned vintage tie
off-white silk shirt
brown tweed jacket
black wool pants
black ankle-boots
pearl stud earrings
gold mesh bracelet

✿ red and black retro-print necktie
white oversized silk shirt
black men's wool vest
black pin-striped trousers
black suede high-heeled loafers
black nylon tote bag

✿ yellow, blue, and white necktie, loosely knotted
white long-sleeved men's-tailored shirt
oversized turquoise V-necked cardigan
white linen full pants with narrow cuffs
blue and yellow argyle socks
black-and-white two-tone oxfords
pearl stud earrings
white cotton duck tote bag

✿ purple and white necktie
white cotton men's-tailored shirt with French cuffs
black V-necked cashmere sweater
black trousers
black cowboy belt

black-and-white polka dot socks
black suede loafers
diamond stud earrings
rhinestone cuff links
black polo coat
purple leather gloves
black tote bag

NEWSBOY CAP

The oversized soft crown and small visor
was the emblematic hat of the struggling
young boy (think Jackie Coogan in
The Kid), especially during the Great
Depression. It has been the traditional
English working man's cap—as much a
mark of class as an accent or address.
Worn by a child, the too-big cap produced an air of cocky vulnerability. The
newsboy cap reappeared as a countercul-
ture statement among English rock stars
in the 1960s, and was worn equally by
men and women. Made of velvet, wool,
or tweed, the slightly droopy cap has a
youthful, jaunty charm.

How to Wear a Newsboy Cap

✿ **brown tweed newsboy cap**
  oatmeal-flecked oversized roll-neck
    sweater
  brown corduroy pants
  brown paisley socks
  brown high-heeled oxfords

✿ **black wool newsboy cap**
  off-white oversized sweater
  black skinny pants
  black Doc Martens
  diamond stud earrings

✿ **black and white tweed newsboy cap**
  white turtleneck sweater
  black cigarette pants
  black ballet flats
  black leather jacket

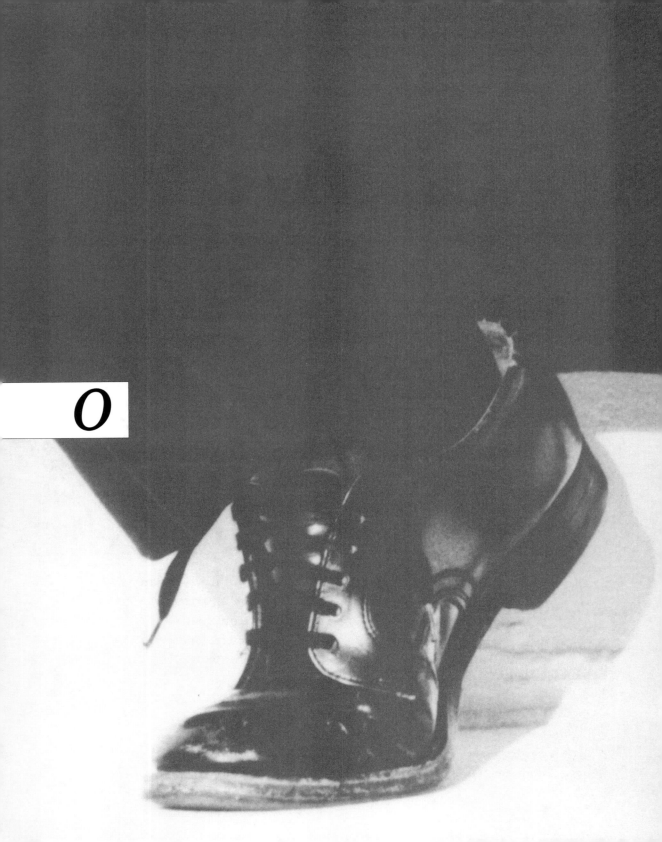

O

OPALS

Opals are intense. These are not quietly elegant stones that gently blend. Opals are in-your-face, demanding attention. And they usually get it.

There are three primary varieties—milky white opals found in Mexico, Czechoslovakia, and Australia that are not rare; expensive, uncommon black opals that actually range in color from electric blue to black; and the prized fire opals—the only true orange stone found in nature. All three forms of opals share a unique feature—an internal light show of colors that shift and sparkle.

Opals are dressy stones that work best with gabardine, velvet, and silk clothing. If you're planning to wear casual sweaters, pants, or tweeds, leave your opals at home. Keep in mind that opals are particularly fragile. They are brittle stones that tend to scratch, crack, and dry out, and they benefit from contact with body oils and moisture. Opal rings, while quite popular, are at high risk for damage. Save these rings for evenings out, rather than situations where you will be using your hands a lot.

How to Wear Opals

❀ **white opal bracelet**
   black linen shift
   bone and black Chanel shoes
   gold hoop earrings
   black nylon tote bag

❀ **white opal and diamond earrings**
   black wool coatdress
   black sheer panty hose
   black suede slingback shoes
   red quilted suede shoulder bag
      on chain

❀ **fire opal earrings**
   rust linen shift
   brown suede sandals
   gold cuff bracelet
   crocheted shoulder bag

ARE OPALS BAD LUCK?

A symbol of fidelity and faith, opals have been popular since the Middle Ages. In the 19th-century best-selling novel "Anne of Geierstein" by Sir Walter Scott, an ill-fated heroine received an opal before her untimely death. As a result, a shadow was cast on the opal in popular opinion, but as time passed the shadow lifted and even the superstitious Queen Victoria continued to give opal jewelry to valued friends and family.

✿ **black opal and diamond earrings**
  black wool suit
  white silk shirt
  black suede pumps
  gold wristwatch
  black Chanel bag

OXFORDS

For centuries oxfords were a sign of casual, even cheeky independence. Originally developed for 17th-century Oxford University students, this low-cut lace-up was a clear break with the boot-shoe styles that had dominated men's footwear for centuries. After World War I returning soldiers, eager to forget every-thing military, abandoned boots and finally made oxfords respectable. In the 1930s style icons such as Katharine Hepburn and Marlene Dietrich wore oxfords and started a trend for women that is still popular.

Oxfords can be worn with pants and argyle socks for a classic tailored look, with long skirts and chunky socks for great casual cold-weather style, and with leggings and a long jacket in a distinctly downtown attitude.

Recently oxfords have crossed fashion boundaries from classic to trendy with a work boot look of lugged soles or thicker soles. Paired with short skirts and tights or baggy wide-wale corduroy overalls, these oxfords have a whole new genera-tion of fans.

THE ULTIMATE OXFORD

Despite a personality that is as English as kippers and crumpets, the most coveted oxfords are made in France by J.M. Weston. Since the turn of the century this exclusive Parisian shoemaker has been crafting superb oxfords for the rich and famous. Their distinctive square-toe shape echoes the chunky French work shoe, rather than the more pointed English walking shoe.

Individually hand-sewn, they are available ready-made or can be custom designed in a range of styles, colors, and leathers. Well-known "Westie" wearers reportedly include Tom Cruise, Christie Brinkley, Lauren Hutton, Melanie Griffith, and make-up artist Bobbi Brown.

How to Wear Oxfords

✿ **black oxfords**
  gray pantsuit
  white notched-collar silk shirt
  cream, gray, and yellow cashmere socks
  antique gold earrings
  pearl necklace

✪ **brown oxfords**
    bone silk and cashmere turtleneck
    brown tweed pants
    brown alligator belt
    brown and cranberry paisley socks
    gold earrings
    gold "San Marco" link bracelet

✪ **black thick-soled oxfords**
    black oversized roll-neck pullover
    black short skirt
    black opaque tights
    silver box-cut drop earrings
    silver pendant on a black silk cord
    thick silver chain bracelet

✪ **black lug-soled oxfords**
    white T-shirt
    blue denim shirt
    blue jeans
    black and white animal-print socks
    black nylon backpack

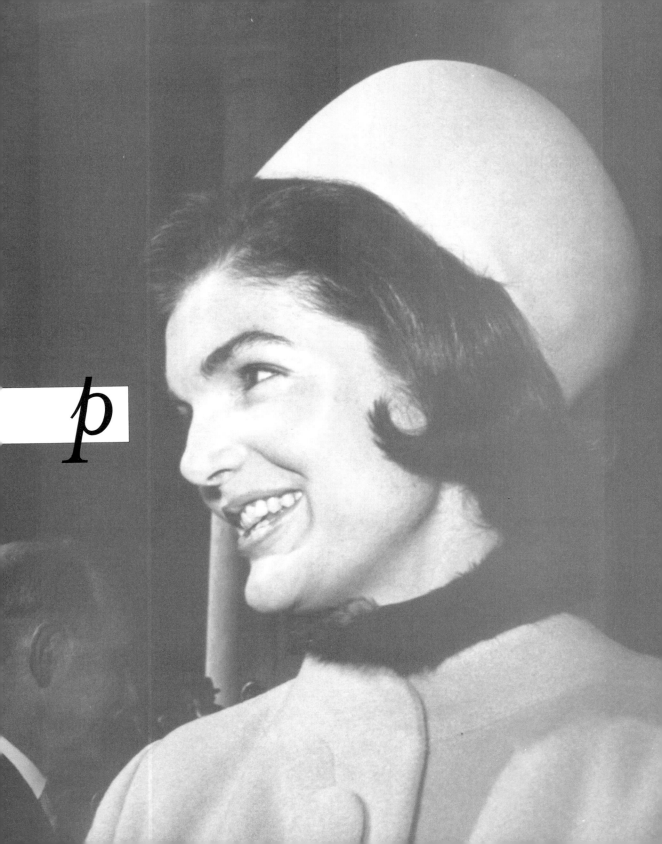

p

PANAMA HAT

The first thing that you should know about the Panama hat is that it is not made in Panama. Crafted in Peru and Ecuador, it was introduced to the United States by sailors returning from Latin America. It became socially acceptable when it was worn by President Theodore Roosevelt to inspect the building of the Panama Canal.

Panama hats are made of finely woven straw and are soft, lightweight, and durable. It is a fairly large hat designed to offer maximum comfort in tropical weather. The high crown circulates the air while the wide brim shades the face and neck. Because of its size, the

Panama hat looks best if you are 5 feet 5 inches or taller. Petite features and forms will probably be happier with a smaller-scale straw hat such as a BOATER or BRETON.

How to Wear a Panama Hat

✿ **natural Panama hat**
  bone silk notched-collar shirt
  bone pleated linen pants
  bone and brown saddle shoes
  white crew socks
  pearl stud earrings

✿ **natural Panama hat**
  bone linen shirt
  tobacco suede wrap skirt
  brown alligator flat sandals
  ivory earrings
  ivory and silver bracelet
  SPF-15 sunscreen

✿ **natural Panama hat**
  bikini bathing suit
  thong sandals
  straw bag

✿ **natural Panama hat**
  white tank top
  blue-and-white-striped cotton shirt
    worn as a jacket
  white knee-length linen shorts
  white slip-on sneakers
  pearl stud earrings
  blue and white cotton boat tote bag

PANTY HOSE

The one-piece sheer panty-and-stocking combination may well be the most popular accessory introduced in the past forty years. Panty hose appeared in the 1950s to an unimpressed public. Then the ultra-thin model Twiggy strutted out in an ultra-short miniskirt. With skirts shorter than most stockings, women abandoned their girdles and garters for the stretchable one-piece hosiery. Even after skirts lengthened, women choose the ease and freedom of panty hose over conventional nylon stockings. Free of buckles, straps, and snaps, women bought panty hose for all skirt lengths.

As hosiery yarns became more sophisticated, different weights of legwear were introduced. Sheers are perfect for business attire in the daytime and are formal and dressy for evening—especially with accents such as a row of rhinestones around the ankle. Thicker hose or opaque tights are usually more casual.

How to Wear Panty Hose

✿ **brown sheer diamond-patterned panty hose**
  black wool suit
  chocolate suede pumps with
    chunky heels
  gold and pearl earrings
  black Kelly bag

✿ black sheer panty hose
black wool suit
silk Dalmatian-printed blouse
black 3-inch pumps
gold button earrings
gold and enamel bracelet

✿ cream sheer
point d'esprit **panty hose**
pink short linen shift
cream and black Chanel-style pumps
pearl earrings
small bone linen shoulder bag

✿ black lace panty hose
black short velvet A-line shift
black silk 3-inch pumps
diamond stud earrings
diamond and pearl bracelet

✿ grape opaque ribbed tights
gray cashmere turtleneck
gray short flannel skirt
grape suede Gucci-style loafers
silver earrings
silver chain bracelets
Cartier-style tank wristwatch

PANTY HOSE TIP SHEET

- DENIER is the number that is used to define the thickness of a fiber and is seen as sheerness or opacity of the hosiery. The higher the denier number, the more opaque the panty hose. For example, sheer dressy hose is 14 denier, while opaque hose is 40 denier.
- LYCRA (the Dupont trade name for spandex) is a fiber that can provide stretch and recovery in all directions. It improves fit and prevents bagging and sagging.
- MICROFIBER—most legwear are made from fibers that are the diameter of the human hair.

Microfibers are 60 times finer than human hair or silk. With the ultra-thin microfibers, manufacturers can create sheer yet strong and flexible legwear.
- TACTEL combines microfiber sheerness with lycra flexibility.
- NYLON has been used since 1935 in everything from parachutes to panty hose to artificial heart valves. It was the first sheer flexible legwear fiber and is still used in combination with newer fibers.
- CONTROL-TOP panty hose combines legwear with a gentle, built-in girdle.

✿ **navy sheer panty hose**
    navy suit
    navy pumps
    pearl and gold earrings
    double-strand pearl necklace
    navy quilted shoulder bag

PEARLS

It is hard to think of another accessory that is as flattering and available as the pearl. Real, cultured, or faux, its luminous light enhances women of any size, age, or coloring. Pearls can be worn with equal ease with casual sportswear, tailored business clothes, and elegant evening wear. Pearls are generous with their beauty, sharing their luminous light with your skin and hair. They are the ultimate team players of accessories, selflessly complementing rather than demanding attention.

Pearls are created when a small foreign object (like a grain of sand) drifts into the shell of an oyster or mussel. To ease the discomfort of the intruder, the mollusk secretes a white crystalline substance, called *nacre*, to coat the irritant. Layering of this luminous material on the grain of sand eventually produces a pearl. In real pearls, the irritants sweep into the shell

PEARL TIP SHEET

- CULTURED PEARLS: Using a technique developed by Kokichi Mikimoto in the 1930s, cultured pearls are produced in the Akoya oysters that live in the shallow ocean waters off Japan. They are seen in a range of whites and grays, but always ask if the color is natural (good) or treated (less good). The best cultured pearls are formed around tiny grains or beads that are allowed to develop many layers of natural nacre. The less-expensive cultured pearls are made with small glass balls, which need far fewer layers of nacre to form a pearl.
- REAL PEARLS: Always rare and expensive, they can only be distinguished from cultured pearls by X ray.
- MABE PEARLS: These pearls are formed on the shell of the oyster. Round or teardrop-shaped, they are smooth on one side and irregular on the other. Grown on Mabe oysters, they are usually used as earrings.
- SOUTH SEA PEARLS: Big, beautiful, and rare, South Sea pearls are produced in an oyster that can be as large as a dinner plate. Ranging from 10 mm (the size of a large pea) to 20 mm (a small olive), the finest South Sea pearls are perfectly round, silvery white, and completely smooth. The newest South Sea pearls are luminous yellow and were born to be worn by blondes.
- TAHITIAN BLACK PEARLS: Harvested from the black-lipped oyster that lives only in the waters of Polynesia, Tahitian black pearls range in color from medium gray to charcoal black. About the same size as South Sea pearls, they are found in both round and teardrop

from the ocean floor. In cultured pearls, a small bead is inserted into the oyster and allowed to mature. After 2–3 years the oysters are harvested and the pearls are removed. Only X rays can tell the difference between cultured and natural pearls, which are over 10 times more expensive than their hand-made cousins.

The finest pearls are perfectly round with a smooth, unblemished surface. Both natural and cultured pearls come in a range of colors from silvery white to glowing charcoal black. The most desirable (and costly) color for the classic string of pearls is a pink-hued white called *roseate,* which is famous for warm-

shapes. Tahitian pearls are used in solitaire rings and earrings, and are often combined with diamonds.

- IMITATION OR FAUX PEARLS: These are created by dipping little glass balls into an iridescent solution that includes fish scales and oyster fluids. Although they are the least expensive pearls, it takes a magnifying glass to differentiate good quality fakes from cultured or real pearls.
- BIWA PEARLS: Small and irregularly shaped, they are found naturally in Oriental freshwater mussels. Also called Japanese freshwater pearls, they come in many shades of white, pink, and gray in square, round, and oval shapes.
- KESHI PEARLS: Irregularly shaped white and gray pearls, they are the byproducts of cultured pearl production. They are attached to the sides of the oyster shells and are now used for interesting modern jewelry design.
- AMERICAN NATURAL PEARLS: Grown in American freshwater mussels, these white oval and lumpy pearls are used mainly in Native American jewelry.
- BAROQUE PEARLS: This is a term given to real, cultured, or fake pearls with a lumpy shape and bumpy surface. They look a lot better than they sound and are worn in earrings, necklaces, bracelets, and solitaire rings.
- MAJORCA: These pearls have never seen the inside of an oyster. The Cadillac of imitation pearls, they are composed of small handblown glass beads dipped 28 times in a patented (and secret) mixture of fish scales and oyster saliva. They are sold in a variety of pearl sizes and colors. Frequently they are more expensive than poor-quality cultured pearls.

ing up pale or yellow skin tones. Silvery or creamy white pearls cool down and soften ruddy, rough complexions.

It probably does not come as much of a surprise that as pearls get bigger, their cost grows too. The average pearl ranges from 4 mm to 9 mm—the size of a peppercorn to the diameter of a mature green pea. Over 10 mm, the price soars for both cultured and natural pearls. In a necklace the pearls are usually graduated slightly in size to drape better around the neck.

How to Wear Pearls

❂ **small pearl stud earrings**
gray long-sleeved turtleneck or
    polo-style sweater
gray flannel pants
black and white patterned socks
black Belgian loafers
square wristwatch with black band
black Bugatti bag

❂ **one black pearl stud earring and
one white pearl stud earring**
white T-shirt
black wool jeans
black short boots
black leather jacket

❂ **pearl choker**
red linen shift
black slingback pumps
two gold bangle bracelets
black small box bag

❂ **matinee-length pearl necklace**
black pantsuit
bone silk shirt
black sheer panty hose
black Chanel flats
diamond stud earrings

❂ **pearl and diamond earrings**
black short velvet shift
black sheer panty hose
black satin slingback pumps

❂ **large faux pearl cuff bracelet**
pink mid-calf linen shift
bone and black Chanel-style flats
small gold hoop earrings
black straw tote bag

❂ **gray pearl stud earrings**
black velvet sheath
black satin high-heeled sandals
red and gold minaudière

❂ **16-inch double-strand
pearl necklace**
red cashmere sweater set
gray flannel pants
black suede loafers
diamond stud earrings

❂ **pearl cluster earrings**
❂ **pearl and diamond bracelet**
black wool fitted suit
cream satin blouse
black sheer panty hose
black silk shoes
black silk envelope bag

❂ **baroque pearl cuff bracelet**
white T-shirt
blue denim overalls
white high-heeled sneakers

❂ **gold and pearl earrings**
❂ **double-strand pearl
necklace**
pink linen skirt suit
pale-toned sheer panty hose

bone and black
Chanel-style pumps
black Chanel-style bag

❀ **single strand of pearls**
navy pantsuit
white T-shirt
navy Gucci-style loafers
gold earrings
gold chain bracelets

PENDANT

More than just decoration, pendants have always been a way of carrying along personal histories and beliefs. Early animal pendants were symbols of fertility, medieval pendants held devotional relics such as sand from the Holy Land, and Victorian pendants were romantic love tokens.

Pendants bridge communication gaps by providing people with a socially acceptable reason to open a conversation. Clearly visible, they give people clues to your personality. For example, a heart-shaped pendant implies that you are sentimental, while an angular silver one can indicate a downtown sensibility. Depending on your body shape and clothing, the pendant should fall midway between your breast line and waist.

Be aware that swinging on the end of a long chain, the pendant takes a lot of abuse when it knocks against desks and tables. Gold, silver, and copper pendants have the best chance to avoid damage. You'll need to be careful with those made from pottery, shells, or stone.

How to Wear a Pendant

❀ **oval silver locket** on 30-inch chain or black velvet cord
gray cropped turtleneck
black mid-calf wool skirt
black granny boots
marcasite earrings

❀ **3-inch gold heart** on 24-inch chain
navy pantsuit
white silk notched-collar shirt
bone ribbed trouser socks
black Belgian loafers
garnet and gold earrings
chunky gold chain bracelet
black leather tote bag

❁ **shell edged in silver** on
    30-inch silver chain
    olive green mid-calf linen shift
    taupe woven slides
    ivory earrings
    silver bangle bracelets
    natural straw tote bag

PICTURE HAT

This is a hat that flatters women—all ages, all shapes, all sizes. The straw picture hat has a brim that is larger than a boater but smaller than a cartwheel hat. Named "picture" because it frames the face, this hat is a wearable symbol of romance. In movies and TV it is worn back from the face to avoid unflattering shadows that are magnified by a camera. In real life, pull the picture hat down lower to highlight your eyes and "erase" fine lines and wrinkles.

A picture hat works beautifully with pretty, flowered dresses or casually elegant linen pants and silk shirts. Plain or decorated with a small corsage of flowers on the crown, the picture hat can also be the perfect finish for an elegant linen or silk suit or dress. An added bonus, the loose crown of a picture hat does not leave "hat hair." If you want to take it off and carry the hat (a charming touch), your hair will still have its natural line and body.

How to Wear a Picture Hat

❁ **natural large straw picture hat**
    white tank top
    banana yellow linen pants
    fishermen's sandals
    pearl stud earrings
    shell bracelet

❁ **black straw picture hat**
    black and white print short silk dress
    sheer panty hose
    black spike heels
    pearl cluster earrings
    black patent leather shoulder bag
        on a chain

❁ **natural straw picture hat**
    flowered mid-calf slip dress
    bone ballet flats
    pearl drop earrings
    bone crocheted bag

❁ **natural straw picture hat** with
    small flower corsage
    ice blue silk skirt suit
    sheer panty hose
    bone slingback spike heels
    aquamarine and pearl earrings
    pearl bracelet
    bone envelope bag

PILLBOX HAT

Originally worn by Greta Garbo in the 1932 film *As You Desire Me,* this round brimless hat has fashion "legs." A hat classic, pillbox hats have been popular due in large part to its hair-friendly shape. The pillbox can sit comfortably on top of both sleek and full hairstyles without disrupting their lines.

Pillbox hats are found in felt, velvet, and straw. Smaller models work beautifully with petite women, while larger styles are best for women over 5 feet 5 inches. This is not an assertive hat. Rather than adding its own dynamics, the pillbox is an excellent finish to an elegant coat or suit. It is good choice for a non-hat-wearer who needs to wear one for a special occasion.

PIN

Pins originated for the most pragmatic of reasons—early man needed something to fashion together skins used for clothing. When garments began to be sewn, rather than draped, the big pin evolved into the decorative brooch while the smaller pins (½ inch to 1 inch) were frequently used to attach collars, cuffs, and scarves to a garment. For example, the 19th-century woman used dainty gold and enamel pins to secure equally dainty lingerie, while the slightly larger bar pin held a lace collar to a shirt or dress.

THE PRESIDENTIAL PILLBOX

Halston crafted a bone wool pillbox hat for Jacqueline Kennedy to wear at her husband's presidential inauguration in 1960. Not a regular hat wearer, she found the shape so flattering that it became her signature hat for many official functions.

In contemporary clothes, little pins look charming worn singly on the collar of a turtleneck or blouse. Groups of small pins are enchanting on the shoulders of a sweater or jacket. These pin clusters should be linked by subject (e.g., butterflies, stars), styles (e.g., Edwardian lingerie pins), or material (e.g., copper, marcasite).

How to Wear a Pin

◉ **cluster of marcasite pins**
    worn on shoulder
    gray crew-neck sweater
    gray flannel trousers
    gray ribbed trouser socks
    black Belgian loafers
    diamond stud earrings

◉ **gold bow pin** worn
    on lapel
    black skirt suit
    white silk blouse
    black sheer panty hose
    black spike heels
    gold and pearl earrings
    gold "San Marco" chain bracelet

◉ **gold flower pin** worn on
    side of neckline
    red linen shift
    black patent leather slingback pumps
    pearl stud earrings
    gold bangle bracelet
    black quilted shoulder bag

◉ **silver bar pin on collar**
    black turtleneck
    black trousers
    black-and-white
      polka-dot socks
    black suede loafers
    silver earrings
    silver cuff bracelet

◉ **cluster of flower pins**
    worn on shoulder
    navy skirt suit
    white silk shirt
    navy sheer panty hose
    navy 2-inch pumps
    small gold hoop earrings

◉ **angel pin** worn at the top
    of one shoulder
    pale blue slip dress
    cream suede open-toed
      platform shoes
    pastel carved Lucite bangle bracelet
    bone crocheted shoulder bag

◉ **tiny vintage rhinestone pins**
    scattered on shoulder
    pale pink cashmere cardigan
      sweater opened at neck
    cream chiffon oblong scarf
      crisscrossed in front and
      tucked into sweater
    gray flannel pants
    gray ribbed trouser socks
    dark gray suede loafers

PUMPS

Pumps are designed to stay on the foot without laces or buckles. These closed-toed slip-on classics earned their name from the "plump, plump" sound they made on stone palace floors. Also known as court shoes, pumps were traditionally worn with floor-length formal clothing. When Chanel paired black pumps with casual knee-length skirts, they were considered daring and sexy as they bared a heretofore unexposed part of the body—the top of the foot. Since the 1930s, pumps in varying toe shapes and heel heights have been a fashion constant.

Times and tastes change, and in an era of lip rings and belly-baring midriff tops, pumps are considered shy, somewhat self-effacing shoes. In $1/2$-inch to $2^{1}/_{2}$-inch heels, this shoe takes a background position behind all the other elements of an outfit.

Choose a pump that flatters both the proportions of your foot and clothing silhouette. For example, with a longer and fuller skirt or dress, choose pumps with a lower heel. Short suits and dresses look beautiful with higher heels. A pair of black calf pumps can be a much-used staple of your wardrobe, so choose the best quality that you can afford.

How to Wear Pumps

✿ **black low-heeled pumps**
   black sweater set
   black mid-calf pleated skirt
   black opaque panty hose
   small silver hoop earrings
   silver cuff bracelet

✿ **black mid-heel pumps**
   black fine-gauge turtleneck
   black-and-white-checked wool short
      slim skirt
   black semi-opaque panty hose
   onyx and gold earrings
   pearl, onyx, and gold double-strand
      bracelet

✿ **black 2- to 3-inch patent leather pumps**
   red wool suit
   black sheer panty hose
   opal and diamond earrings
   gold chain-link bracelet
   suede mini-backpack

✿ **gray suede 3-inch pumps**
   pink boucle wool suit
   gold and pearl earrings
   double-strand pearl bracelet
   gray quilted Chanel-style
      shoulder bag

STILETTO HEELS: THE X-RATED SHOE

There are high-heeled pumps and then there are stilettos—high, thin, spindly heels that are difficult to walk in and incontestably sexy. The raised arch of the stiletto shoe throws the spine into an S-curve, emphasizing the breasts and bottom. Your walk changes as your hips swivel and roll to take the pressure off the instep. Your legs seem to undergo a metamorphosis: ankles and calves slim down and legs take on new curves.

The gold standard for contemporary stiletto heels are made by Manolo Blahnik. With almost-gravity-defying narrow heels, these elegant, sexy shoes are actually a little easier to walk in than they look. They are the perfect shoe for after-five dressy clothing, rather than for the average workday.

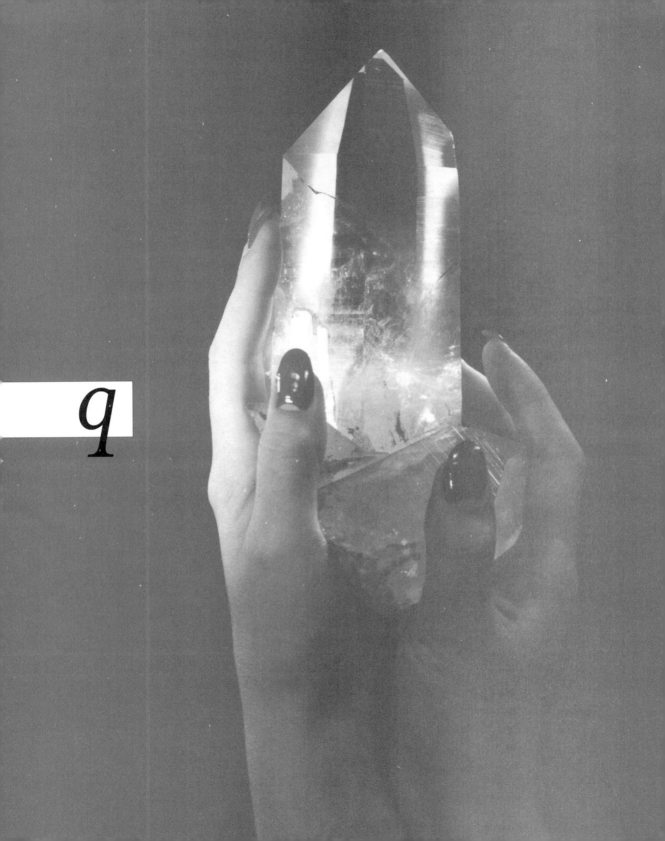

q

QUARTZ

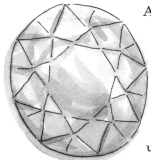

All gemstones are crystalline in nature, but what we call crystals are usually a variety of quartz. Earrings and amulets made with quartz are popular New Age accessories. According to believers, crystals have the power to focus energy and bring health and happiness to the wearer. White crystal (also known as rock crystal) is believed to have general healing properties while rose quartz is said to promote love and kindness. Smoky quartz is reputed to neutralize negative influences.

You will find crystals strung into beads and mounted in jewelry still in their rough natural state—this is because psychics believe that uncut crystals have the strongest natural powers.

How to Wear Quartz

✿ **rose quartz pendant** on 24-inch
silver chain
white turtleneck
black long pullover
black leggings
white crew socks
black suede loafers
silver dome earrings

✿ **multiple-strand rose quartz choker**
gray cashmere crew-neck sweater
gray flannel pants
gray pin-striped socks
black suede loafers
small silver hoop earrings
silver cuff bracelet

✿ **smoky quartz crystal** on bone
silk cord
tan mid-calf linen shift
brown alligator sandals
straw bag

r

RHINESTONES

These foil-backed pieces of faceted glass offer the sparkle if not the brilliance of genuine diamonds. Worn for centuries by the royals, it took the unusual combination of a great designer and an economic catastrophe to place rhinestones around the necks and arms of the average woman. In the 1930s Chanel introduced large bold pieces of rhinestone-studded costume jewelry. To Depression-weary women these fabulous pieces promised a bright new future in a frightening, dark time. The Depression ended over fifty years ago, but rhinestones, both clear and colored, have remained part of the fashion landscape.

There are two basic ways to wear fake gems. For impact, attitude, and sparkle, use them in large, obviously costume pieces. Alternatively, worn in tiny discreet doses like stud earrings and narrow bracelets, rhinestones can pass for expensive and genuine gems.

Whichever style you chose to wear, treat your rhinestones gently. Unlike diamonds, which are one of the hardest substances on earth, rhinestones are fragile. Their metal backing tends to wear away from routine wear or moisture. If this foil becomes damaged, the rhinestone loses its sparkle. Unfortunately it is almost impossible to restore, and once it is gone, the rhinestone looks like a piece of dirty, dull glass.

How to Wear Rhinestones

❂ **large rhinestone bow brooch** worn on shoulder
black pantsuit
white silk shirt
black satin stiletto heels
diamond stud earrings
black and silver minaudière
  or evening bag

"REAL" RHINESTONES

Rhinestones at one time referred to the rock crystals that were found at the bottom of the Rhine River in Germany. Rock crystals are still used in costume jewelry, providing an intense sparkle. More expensive than glass rhinestones, these pieces retain their brilliance far longer than their foil-backed cousins.

✿ **rhinestone stud earrings**
    black velvet sheath
    black satin pumps
    double-strand pearl necklace
    marcasite wristwatch
    black satin shoulder bag

✿ **pearl and rhinestone button earrings**
    red fitted wool suit
    black sheer panty hose
    black calf pumps
    black Kelly bag

✿ **rhinestone stud earrings**
✿ **vintage rhinestone hat pin**
    worn on jacket lapel
    white linen shirt
    tweed blazer
    blue jeans
    brown leather belt

    brown paisley socks
    brown suede loafers
    brown pigskin Bugatti bag

✿ **black and clear rhinestone cuff bracelet**
✿ panty hose with **rhinestone ankle trim**
    black velvet stretch top
    black pleated gabardine pants
    black satin pumps
    pearl stud earrings
    red minaudière

RING

Rings are charged with personal significance. Throughout history rings have been used to indicate rank, confer high office, invoke magic powers, carry poison, commemorate events, or seal a marriage.

Perhaps because rings are so personal and so emblematic of self we tend to wear the same ones year after year. During high school and college we wear school rings. A few years later we slip on engagement and wedding bands. Although we may acquire new rings, this is often the accessory that spends its life in a little box in your drawers. It almost seems as if it is not worth the effort to change rings for different looks. Not true. Although small in size compared to a hat or scarf, rings can offer a subtle yet distinct finish to a look.

Rings come in sizes, but any metal ring can be made larger or smaller. Small hands generally look better with narrow, dainty rings, while broad bands and large stones offer the best proportions for larger hands.

How to Wear a Ring

✿ **opal and diamond dinner ring**
black short velvet sheath
black sheer panty hose
black and gold Chanel slingback shoes
black satin envelope bag

✿ **pearl ring**
white silk shirt
navy blazer
gray flannel pants
black ribbed trouser socks

THE SIX BASIC TYPES OF RINGS

1. **SIGNET: an emblematic ring etched with heraldic design or initials. Created originally to signify clan or family, it is an elegant tailored touch of gold or silver.**

2. **DINNER: a gold or platinum band with gemstones or pearls, it is usually accented with diamonds. Not infrequently the stones will be somewhat larger than in a ring used for day wear.**

3. **WEDDING: a gold or platinum band. It can be plain, etched with a design, or garnished with diamonds.**

4. **ENGAGEMENT: traditionally inlaid with a single faceted diamond. The sapphire and diamond ring of Diana, the Princess of Wales, launched a new trend. Rings that feature a sapphire or ruby are now rising in popularity, especially for second (or third) marriages.**

5. **CLASS: thick and chunky, with a large inexpensive stone, the style is modified slightly for different schools. Hearty and masculine, it blends beautifully with backpacks, sweatshirts, and term papers.**

6. **ETHNIC: constructed of beautiful natural materials (ivory, amber, and tortoiseshell, for example), they add a wonderful touch of texture to summery clothes.**

black Belgian loafers
gold knot earrings
gold charm bracelet
black Bugatti bag

✿ **gold signet ring**
bone silk shirt
brown tweed jacket
blue jeans
cranberry and brown paisley socks
brown alligator-patterned loafers
small gold hoop earrings

✿ **coral ring**
gray gabardine pantsuit
pale blue shirt with white collar
gray silk trouser socks
black patent leather loafers
coral earrings

✿ **cameo ring**
pink linen shift
bone and black Chanel
   slingback pumps
pearl earrings
pearl bracelet

✿ **ivory ring guards**
brown linen shift
brown fishermen's sandals
ivory earrings
red, green, and bone
   Bakelite bangle bracelets
straw tote bag

✿ **Native American silver and turquoise ring**
black mid-calf linen shift
black mules
large silver earrings
silver cuff bracelet

RUBIES

This deep red July birthstone is the rarest and most valuable of all the gems. Since prehistoric times rubies have been mined in Thailand and Burma. Ancient Indian beliefs held that if a man offered rubies to the gods, he would become a king or emperor in his next life (his future rank depended on the quality of the rubies).

The clear, rich red tones of the ruby are very flattering for all colorings, except ruddy skins and red hair. Rubies warm up pale or yellowish skin tones and enhance most shades of blond, gray, black, and brown hair. They are usually set in gold and work beautifully with polished daytime and after-five clothing.

The fashion impact of rubies has been limited by their scarcity and price. Carat for carat, a ruby can cost three times more than a diamond. Synthetic rubies, developed around the turn of the century, offer the color and sparkle, if not the romance, of the genuine stone.

THE DUCHESS AND THE RUBIES

The Duke of Windsor gave his wife, Wallis, a ruby and diamond necklace for her 40th birthday that contained no fewer than 123 Burmese rubies. The necklace matched two ruby and diamond bracelets, a pair of ruby and diamond earrings, and a set of ruby and diamond hair ornaments that the prince had given her since they had met. The jewels were so elaborate and so extraordinary that columnists described the Duchess as "dripping in rubies."

How to Wear Rubies

❁ **ruby and diamond earrings**
black chiffon dress
black sheer panty hose
black high-heeled satin slingbacks
diamond tennis bracelet
diamond ring

❁ **ruby and gold earrings**
black coatdress
black panty hose
black patent leather Chanel pumps
pearl bracelet
black patent leather envelope bag

❁ **ruby and gold ring**
navy skirt suit
navy sheer panty hose
navy slingback shoes
mabe pearl earrings
navy Chanel shoulder bag

❁ **ruby and diamond bracelets**
black sleeveless velvet dress
black satin mules
diamond and pearl earrings
pearl necklace

S

SADDLE SHOES

These two-toned oxfords first appeared in the 1920s as part of a national passion to forget the horrors of the trenches. In the years following the end of World War I, men and women rushed to enjoy sunny resorts and easygoing sports. From Palm Beach to the French Riviera, the white and tan saddle shoe became the perfect partner for the white flannel slacks and blazers of stylish vacationers. The determinedly casual shoe soon became *the* shoe at Yale and Princeton. For almost 30 years the saddle shoe endured, practically a badge of the American student. Seen as a symbol of the establishment, it was discarded in the social changes of the 1960s and replaced by work boots and running shoes.

The traditional saddle shoe found in men's shoe stores and well-stocked flea markets can add a knowing retro look to pants and jackets. Unusual color combinations, such as pink and green, and saddle shoes with platform or lugged soles, are available from trendier stores and catalogs that are aimed at teenagers.

This shoe still has a big personality. The two-color look will draw immediate attention to your foot. Echo one of the shoes' two colors near your face. Saddle shoes add nostalgia to a pair of traditional khakis, and a bit of irony to a minimalist pantsuit.

How to Wear Saddle Shoes

✿ **brown and white lug-soled saddle shoes**
off-white fishermen's sweater
blue jeans
short white crew socks
pearl stud earrings
red paisley satchel bag

✿ **white and tan saddle shoes**
white short-sleeved polo shirt
khaki pants
white socks
small gold hoop earrings
tan backpack

✿ **white and tan saddle shoes**
off-white fine-gauge crew-neck
tweed jacket
tan gabardine pants
bone cashmere crew socks
gold "shrimp" earrings
paisley scarf

✿ **black and white saddle shoes**
white oxford shirt
yellow cropped Shetland pullover
red boxy waist-length boiled-wool
   jacket with silver buttons
black-and-white-plaid mid-calf
   hip-stitched skirt
yellow cable socks
silver bangle bracelets

❃ **pink and white saddle shoes**
  white sleeveless cotton turtleneck
  pink vintage beaded cardigan
  khaki pants
  white crew socks
  silver stud earrings
  pearl cuff bracelet

❃ **brown and white saddle shoes**
  cream vintage men's gabardine shirt
  brown, cream, and pink argyle vest
  brown tweed jacket
  cream wool trousers
  white crew socks
  pearl stud earrings
  pale pink wool muffler

❃ **black and white saddle shoes**
  white polished cotton shirt with
    French cuffs
  black fitted hip-length jacket
  black narrow pants
  black-and-white polka-dot socks
  pearl stud earrings
  black vintage men's enamel cuff links
  black nylon tote bag

❃ **black and white lug-soled
  saddle shoes**
  black long-sleeved T-shirt
  baggy white overalls
  red socks
  small gold hoop earrings
  black and red argyle muffler
  red leather backpack

SAILOR HAT

There are few hats that connote summer better than a sailor hat. This small white canvas cap with an upturned brim has been part of the uniform of the U.S. Navy since the late 19th century. Cheap and charming, it offers a bit of shade as it adds a sporty finish to shorts and sandals. Sailor hats are particularly wonderful on boats, because if they get wet they take on a floppy charm while wet straw hats just tend to disintegrate. Sailor hats are also made in khaki and camouflage fabrics with the brim turned down. The result is a summer hat with a jungle attitude.

Sailor caps work best on small- to average-sized heads and hairdos. On larger heads or bigger hair, sailor hats tend to perch on top, making you look more like Popeye than you probably planned.

How to Wear a Sailor Hat

✿ **white sailor hat, brim turned down**
   red-and-white-striped boat-neck
      T-shirt
   white pants
   white slip-on Keds
   pearl cuff bracelet

✿ **white sailor hat**
   white T-shirt
   light blue shorts
   flowered flats

✿ **white sailor hat**
   white T-shirt
   flowered cotton overalls
   white espadrilles
   small pearl stud earrings

SANDALS

Sandals are the ultimate warm weather shoe. Light, airy, and designed to be worn without hosiery, they are the perfect accompaniment to summer clothing. They are comfortable and versatile with pants, shorts, casual dresses of all lengths, and, of course, bathing suits.

For the best fit, toes and heels should finish exactly where the sole ends. Thin feet and legs look wonderful in open strappy sandals; heavier feet and legs look better in less revealing sandals, such as open-toe slingbacks. Whatever style you choose, make sure that the heels and soles of your feet are smooth, soft, and free of calluses and dry skin.

How to Wear Sandals

✿ **rubber thongs**
   bathing suit
   terry shorts
   diamond stud earrings
   straw tote bag

✿ **tan sandals**
   pale green mid-calf cotton knit dress
   ivory earrings
   ivory and silver bangle bracelets

✿ **navy woven leather sandals**
   navy mid-calf linen dress
   small gold hoop earrings
   red Bakelite bracelets
   navy straw shoulder bag

✿ **brown woven leather slingback sandals**
   white T-shirt
   brown-and-white-checked pants
   brown wooden cuff bracelets

❁ **bright pink open-toe
slingback sandals**
white short-sleeved mock turtleneck
    sweater
pink and white floral-print slim pants
pearl stud earrings

❁ **white slingback sandals**
blue-and-white-striped
    dress
red Bakelite bracelet
straw tote bag with red cherries
pearl stud earrings

❁ **white sandals with stacked heels**
turquoise raw silk sheath
lime green crew-neck sweater tied
    around shoulders
pearl stud earrings
gold chain-link bracelets

❁ **brown T-strap sandals**
white T-shirt
tan linen overshirt
tan short linen skirt
silver and tortoiseshell earrings
tortoiseshell cuff bracelet
brown linen tote bag

SAPPHIRES

In hues that range from the light blue of
a flawless sky to the velvety color of the
Caribbean, the sapphire has become
synonymous with luminous blue.

Sapphires are either cut and faceted
for sparkle or smoothed into cabochon
stones. In some cases, six striations
appear in a cabochon, forming the
highly prized star sapphire. The birthstone of September, sapphires enhance
and deepen the natural color of blue
eyes. All other shades of eye color look
spectacular with sapphires when worn
with shades of navy or red. Like her sis-
ter stone, the ruby, sapphire is a natural
partner for pearls and diamonds in earrings, bracelets, and pins.

The sapphire is surrounded by a long
history of mystical powers, all of them
good. Ancient civilizations believed it
protected kings from harm and envy.
Queen Elizabeth I, believing they protected her from plots and intrigue, wore
sapphires until the day she died peacefully in her sleep—a distinct rarity for
medieval monarchs. In the theater,
actors maintain that the gem can prevent
stage fright and build confidence.

The finest sapphires are found in Sri
Lanka. Although still expensive, carat
for carat sapphires are the most affordable of the precious stones.

How to Wear Sapphires

✿ **sapphire and diamond earrings**
navy gabardine coatdress
navy sheer panty hose
navy 2-inch heels
pearl bracelet
small navy envelope bag on chain

✿ **sapphire, ruby, and diamond bracelet**
red skirt suit
black sheer panty hose
black patent leather pumps
diamond stud earrings
black patent leather Chanel-style bag

✿ **sapphire cabochon and gold earrings**
navy pantsuit
white silk shirt
navy Chanel-style flats
gold chain bracelet
navy leather bag

✿ **sapphire cabochon earrings**
off-white cashmere twin set
navy pleated trousers
navy Belgian loafers
bone or navy ribbed socks
single-strand pearl necklace

SATCHEL BAG

Reminiscent of a doctor's bag, this flat-bottomed purse is trim yet roomy. The satchel's tailored, conservative style works beautifully with pants, suits, sweaters, and jackets. The rounded sides tend to add too much bulk to dressier suits and silky dresses.

You will find satchels in solid leathers, colorful quilted prints, and sporty canvas. They are held either by small handles or longer straps that hang from the shoulders. The shape and size appeal to women who juggle the responsibilities of career, parenthood, and home. A medium-sized satchel is spacious enough to carry gloves, wallet, a favorite lipstick, an extra diaper, a box of animal crackers, and a compact disc player.

A BAG OF DISTINCTION

The satchel may look like a doctor's bag, but it is actually a smaller version of the wildly popular 19th-century gladstone luggage bag. Named after the four-term British prime minister, William Evert Gladstone, it was the perfect bag for a nation in love with travel. The soft sides and flat bottom could hold everything a man needed to explore the world.

How to Wear a Satchel Bag

❀ **red and white quilted satchel bag**
white T-shirt
denim overalls
white slip-on Keds
red Bakelite bracelet

❀ **luggage tan leather satchel**
cranberry crew-neck
brown plaid pants
brown-tone paisley socks
brown alligator-patterned
    loafers
gold knot earrings
gold chain-link bracelets

❀ **luggage tan leather satchel**
white shirt
navy blazer
blue jeans
cranberry paisley socks
brown suede loafers
pearl stud earrings

SCARF

Scarves are a relatively recent fashion development, usually attributed to the dancer Isadora Duncan. At the turn of the century, audiences were enchanted with the image of the tall, beautiful red-head dancing with long white silk scarves. Couturiers, such as Madame Vionnet, recognizing a good thing when they saw it, quickly added long filmy scarves to their suits and dresses.

In the years that followed, scarves have accompanied different fashion trends. During World War II, women wrapped scarves around their heads to protect their hair (and their lives) when they went to work in the factories to aid the war effort. By the 1950s, scarves were a basic accessory in movies and Brigitte Bardot knotted a small scarf under her chin as a wedding hat.

While scarf fashions continue to change, there have always been basically two shapes—oblong and square.

In silk or wool, a solid color or print pattern, the oblong is a slimming touch of color and movement. These scarves can be simply draped around the neck, tied as a belt, wrapped around a straw hat, or folded into an ascot. The long narrow shape is particularly flattering for the current longer, leaner shape of clothing. A flowered or pleated chiffon oblong adds softness while a silk paisley or geometric pattern brings polish to tailored suits or jackets.

Square scarves can be draped over the

shoulder, knotted into a tie, wrapped around the waist, and wrapped casually around the handle of a handbag. Square scarves work particularly well with the short blocky fashions of the 1960s and '70s and can add elegance and color to tailored suits. Keep in mind that the crisp edges of a square scarf may not work as well with the current longer and looser silhouette.

Scarf designs may seem infinite, but there are actually eight types: floral, geometric, paisley, solids, ethnic, plaid, vintage, and status style (e.g., Hermès or Gucci). There are four types of fabrics: wool, silk, cotton, and chiffon. A flexible scarf wardrobe should include some of each. It is not unusual to keep buying the same type of scarf over and over, and have a drawer full of scarves that work with only one type of clothing. If you like to wear scarves, take an hour to sort them into piles to see where there are repeats and where there is an opportunity to expand your collection.

Silk scarves, like the classic Hermès, possess hard power, commanding center stage in any outfit. Porous and subtle, chiffon scarves have soft power, expressing emotion and possibility, rather than authority.

Much of the advice about scarves has focused on ways to tie them. In general, if you need to follow a blueprint to tie a scarf, you are doing something wrong. The impact of the scarf lies with the color, shape, pattern, and fabric, not on a complicated arrangement.

How to Wear a Scarf

✿ **oblong paisley or lace scarf**
   tucked under jacket collar
brown tweed jacket
taupe gabardine pants
taupe ribbed trouser socks
brown alligator-patterned
   loafers
gold earrings
gold chain bracelets

✿ **Hermès-style scarf** worn
   as belt
white cotton shirt
blue jeans
white Keds
gold earrings
gold chain bracelets

THE POWER OF CHIFFON

When Alfred Hitchcock was shooting a key night scene with Kim Novak in the movie "Vertigo," he positioned her alone against the corner of a plain white building. She had been costumed in a white coat and black turtleneck, and he planned to create tension with the stark juxtapositions of black and white. But the scene wasn't working for Hitch—it was too static. It needed something mysterious, unpredictable. He ordered a long white oblong chiffon scarf from wardrobe. When Novak put on the filmy fabric and it started blowing around her, the scene suddenly came alive with emotion. The master director instinctively knew the difference between hard power and soft power and when each was effective.

✿ **chiffon scarf** wrapped
around a straw hat
white tiny T-shirt
flowered slip dress
white thong sandals
pearl stud earrings
straw tote bag

✿ **scarf with cartoon
characters** tied at the waist
white T-shirt
black jeans

white crew socks
black high-heeled
sneakers

✿ **cranberry cashmere
scarf** looped around
handle of brown bag
cream cashmere sweater
gray flannel pants
black Belgian loafers
gold earrings
gold charm bracelet

✿ **square print scarf** tied loosely
over a low ponytail
black turtleneck sweater
black mid-calf skirt
black cowboy boots
silver "bean" earrings
silver chain bracelet

✿ **square or oblong print scarf**
tied under collar, with knot
below breastbone
white cotton shirt
camel pleated trousers
brown suede loafers
garnet earrings
gold and pearl bracelet
tan raincoat

✿ **long ethnic scarf** flung
around the neck
white T-shirt
denim overalls
white chunky socks
black Doc Martens

✿ **print scarf** wrapped
around neck as a "choker"
men's black V-necked sweater
blue jeans
white crew socks
black suede loafers
gold earrings
gold chain bracelets
black suede mini-backpack

SCRUNCHY

The scrunchy began as a new way to pull little girls' hair back without the tangling and pulling of a bare rubber band. The potential for style propelled the scrunchy out of the playground and onto the streets. Whenever hair became annoying, women of all ages could whip out a scrunchy and wrap it around the hair. Scrunchy styles include conservative black velvet, colorful cotton prints, richly textured beads, and glammy gold lamé. They are the perfect antidote to a bad-hair day, and quickly coordinate your hair with the rest of your look.

How to Wear a Scrunchy

✿ **leopard-print scrunchy**
black short linen shift
black 2-inch slides
small black pearl drop earrings

✿ **black velvet scrunchy**
 red cashmere mock turtleneck
 black pleated trousers
 red and black socks
 black suede loafers
 pearl stud earrings
 pearl cuff bracelet

✿ **natural wooden bead scrunchy**
 olive green mid-calf linen shift
 brown woven slides
 ivory earrings
 amber bracelet
 straw tote bag

✿ **white eyelet scrunchy**
 flowered mid-calf slip dress
 white linen slides
 pearl drop earrings
 straw tote bag

✿ **cartoon-print scrunchy**
 black short-sleeved T-shirt
 white overalls
 black high-heeled sneakers
 red leather fanny pack

SHAWL

Luxurious and colorful, shawls have been worn since the dawn of clothing. However, it was only when French soldiers brought them back for their wives and sweethearts from Egypt at the end of the 18th century that these large wraps became a fashion item. Indian-inspired paisleys and embroidered silk shawls remained a fashion constant for 200 years, even as dress styles changed from full crinoline-lined skirts to narrow Regency gowns and back to the swaying hoopskirt. There were stores devoted just to shawls, and women were judged on their ability to drape and carry a shawl on their bodies.

Beautiful yet practical, shawls are still a relevant fashion accessory. Tossed over a suit (pants- or skirt) they add elegance, texture, and movement to all looks. The cashmere or thin wool shawl folds gracefully around the body without adding bulk. Silk shawls add finish to hot-weather clothes while keeping away the chill of a cool summer evening. Sometimes rather than being content to rest gracefully on our shoulders, large silk scarves tend to slip and slide on the body. If you want to wear a silky fabric, look for styles featuring long fringes that seem to weigh down the fabric, or embroidery, which supplies some traction against your clothing.

THE SWEATER SHAWL

Tying a sweater around your shoulders adds cozy warmth as it frames the face with texture and color. More youthful than a shawl, the sweater tie is a casual, relaxed look that adds charm and move-ment. The best sweaters for tying are cashmere, and it can be a wonderful way to recycle a slightly aging pullover whose color is still luminous. Tossed around your neck, its age seems to disappear.

How to Wear a Shawl

❁ **red cashmere or wool shawl**
  navy pantsuit
  white silk shirt
  navy ribbed trouser socks
  navy suede loafers
  gold earrings
  gold chain bracelets
  navy leather bag

❁ **black velvet burn-out-patterned shawl**
  black long velvet dress
  black sheer panty hose
  black satin 4-inch sandals
  rhinestone earrings

❁ **tan paisley wool or woven silk shawl**
  bone pantsuit
  bone mock turtleneck
  bone patterned trouser socks
  brown alligator shoes
  gold earrings
  brown crystal brooch on lapel

SHELLS

If you own a pair of cowrie shell earrings or a long string of puka shells, chances are that they were acquired during a sunny seaside vacation. Draped on a linen tunic top or worn with a colorful native print skirt, shells seem to be the perfect finish. With thick woolen sweaters or a trim gabardine suit they are less perfect. The delicate colorings and fragile texture need equally organic elements to shine. If you live in a warm, sunny climate, casual shell jewelry can be a popular choice for weekend or recreational wear. In cold regions, reserve them for trips to places with palm trees.

How to Wear Shells

✪ **cowrie shell earrings**
kente cloth mid-calf shift
brown mules or sandals
straw tote bag

✪ **24-inch puka shell necklace**
bone linen tank dress
bone sandals
ivory earrings
straw tote bag

✪ **multiple-strand shell choker**
black linen shift
black straw flats
ivory and silver bangle bracelet
black straw tote bag

✪ **multiple-strand shell bracelet**
white linen shirt
brown linen skirt
alligator-patterned sandals
shell earrings
straw tote bag

THE STATUS SHELL

There is a unique style of shell jewelry that is both elegant and witty. Created by the legendary (and eccentric) designer Fulco, Duke of Verdura, this tropical snail shell is wrapped with gold wire, studded with pearls or gemstones, and worn as an earring. It was a favorite with the Duchess of Windsor, probably because it is a perfect mix of shape and color for tailored suits and dresses. Unlike its more natural cousins, the Verdura shell works for all seasons.

✪ **white shell bracelets**
white tank top
blue and white batik wrap skirt
navy slides
ivory earrings

SHOULDER BAG

Any medium-sized bag with a long matching strap is a shoulder bag. Worn in the early days of World War II, it was designed for women in the military, allowing them to snap off a crisp salute while carrying a purse.

It would be wonderful if shoulder bags came in exact sizes like shoes, but

they don't. If you are shorter than 5 feet 3 inches, the bag should not be $1\frac{1}{2}$ times larger than your head. Taller women can handle bags that are proportionally larger. When searching for a new bag, take time to see how low it hangs against your body. Straps that are too long can be easily shortened by a shoemaker. When the straps are too short, they can be replaced by chain-link strands.

How to Wear a Shoulder Bag

✿ **brown pigskin-pattern shoulder bag**
  off-white fishermen's sweater
  brown corduroy pants
  cranberry and brown paisley socks
  brown suede loafers
  gold heart earrings
  gold bangle bracelets
  olive quilted barn jacket

✿ **black patent leather shoulder bag**
  black skirt suit
  black pumps
  black and white pearl earrings
  gardenia pin on shoulder

✿ **navy shoulder bag**
  navy pantsuit
  off-white turtleneck
  red suede loafers
  gold earrings
  red and navy scarf knotted
    around neck

SILVER

Hammered, polished, beaten, or rolled, silver has always been a runner-up to gold as a jewelry material. Until the 19th century, most silver jewelry consisted of ethnic or peasant pieces made by local and native craftsmen. Luminous and graceful, silver finally came into its own as part of the national celebration that marked the silver jubilee of Queen Victoria's 50-year reign.

Since 1887, silver has continued to be used for beautiful and affordable pins,

THE DIRTY TRUTH ABOUT TARNISHING

The dark discoloration of silver that we take for granted is actually the consequence of the Industrial Revolution. Until the 18th century, city air was fairly clean until factories began to fill the sky with smoke from coal-burning fires. These sulfurous fumes create the chemical reaction that tarnishes silver. To clean silver jewelry, use a liquid silver polish designed just for jewelry. Traditional cream or paste polish formulations are unable to get into tiny chains and carvings, and are difficult to rinse off.

bracelets, rings, earrings, and necklaces. Every era and culture has contributed its own designs. You will find delicate Edwardian necklace styles, chunky Native American rings, hand-tooled Mexican earrings, geometric art deco pins, and Bauhaus-inspired bracelets.

For the best effect, wear one high-profile piece of silver jewelry, backed up with simple complimentary styles. For example, when you wear a large silver Native American brooch on a black jacket, let it be the focus by adding small simple hoop earrings and sleek silver bangles.

How to Wear Silver

◉ **small silver hoop earrings**
◉ **silver link bracelets**
   white cotton shirt
   blue jeans
   western-style belt
   white crew socks
   brown or navy loafers
   brown leather backpack

◉ **silver "bean" earrings**
◉ **silver cuff bracelet**
   black mid-calf linen shift
   black patent leather mules
   black straw tote bag

◉ **silver "X" earrings**
◉ **silver chain-link bracelets**
   gray crew-neck sweater

SILVER TIP SHEET

- **STERLING: pure silver, like pure gold, is too soft to be used alone. Sterling silver is composed of 925 parts per 1,000 of silver and 75 parts of copper.**
- **PLATED: nickel, copper, or stainless steel coated with a layer of silver.**
- **OPENWORK: pierced metal designs.**
- **REPOUSSÉ: raised designs produced by hammering or punching (also known as embossing).**
- **INLAY: ornamentation with another material such as ivory, shell, stone, or glass.**

---

   gray flannel pants
   black and gray argyle socks
   black suede Belgian loafers
   black bag

◉ **square silver earrings**
◉ **silver link bracelets**
   white T-shirt
   black wool jacket
   blue jeans
   white crew socks
   black suede loafers
   black Bugatti bag

❀ **filigree silver necklace**
❀ **assorted delicate silver rings**
    black mid-calf velour empire dress
    black opaque panty hose
    black ballet flats

❀ **small silver hoop earrings**
❀ **stack of silver ethnic bangle
    bracelets**
    black crew-neck sweater
    black pants
    black trouser socks
    black patent leather loafers

❀ **silver hoop earrings**
❀ **ivory and silver bangle bracelet**
    white T-shirt
    black mid-calf wool shift
    black opaque panty hose
    black quilted Chanel-style flats

❀ **silver earrings**
❀ **silver cuff bracelet**
    white T-shirt
    blue denim shirt
    black blazer
    black cigarette pants
    black-and-white polka-dot socks
    black suede loafers

SNEAKERS

Sneakers are the most democratic of footwear, worn by men, women, and children in every corner of the world.

Appearing in 1875, they were dubbed sneakers because of their silent footfall. Sneakers, initially designed for croquet, were the first shoes to take advantage of the new vulcanized process that hardened rubber without losing its bounce.

L $1.89 12½ to 3   M $1.69 8 to 12   N $2.29

The first mass-marketed model was called Keds (a combination of the words kids and peds—Latin for feet).

For about ninety years sneaker styles remained basically unchanged, until a committed track coach at the University of Oregon began to look for a way to improve traction for his runners without using spikes. According to legend, coach Bill Bowerman was inspired by the pattern on his waffle iron. He poured liquid urethane into a hot waffle iron, let it cook, and produced the first modern sole of a running shoe. Adding a wedged heel, a cushion midsole, and a nylon body, he called the shoe Nike, after the goddess of victory.

Today more than 90% of people who wear athletic shoes use them for casual wear rather than sport. Just as Englishmen in the 19th century were criticized for wearing boots when they never rode horses, people wear athletic shoes when they have no plans of running a 10K race or playing mixed doubles. Comfortable and affordable, they have become icons of American leisure time. The multicolored, high-tech athletic shoe is essential for high-performance sports, but you will probably get more fashion mileage from solid-toned sneakers. Look for traditional, platform, and high-heeled sneakers in white, black, and red. You can find them in a range of fabrics, including canvas, leather, nylon, and suede.

SNEAKER TIP SHEET

- **RUNNING SHOES: must provide cushioning to absorb impact. Look for midsoles of polyurethane, as well as a heel counter.**
- **TENNIS SHOES: side-to-side movement calls for shoe stabilizers with fiberboard that run the length of the shoe. Plastic stabilizing straps attached to the eyelets provide support during lunges and quick stops.**
- **AEROBIC SHOES: multidirectional movement needs features that include contoured midsoles, wider outersole base, heel stabilizers, and adequate cushioning.**
- **WALKING SHOES: a long steady pace calls for a removable inner sole that should be replaced every 500 miles. Leather uppers and mesh sides offer ventilation and flexibility.**

How to Wear Sneakers

❋ **white high-heeled sneakers**
red twin set
white cotton trousers
large pearl cuff bracelet
red leather fanny pack

✿ **white sneakers**

white baseball cap

sleeveless oxford shirt

tan shorts

pearl stud earrings

silver chain bracelets

✿ **black high-heeled sneakers**

yellow jacket with black velvet collar

black-and-white-checked
   mid-calf skirt

red and black Bakelite bracelet

✿ **red high-top sneakers**

black turtleneck

white overalls

black and red Bakelite earrings

red fanny pack

✿ **white sneakers**

blue-and-white polka-dot mid-calf
   shirtwaist dress

white short anklets

pearl stud earrings

✿ **white sneakers**

white fishermen's sweater

blue jeans

white crew socks

small gold earrings

brown leather backpack

SNOOD

This knit or mesh net covers the hair at the back of the head and has been worn on and off for centuries. In 1939 the Hollywood fashion designer Adrian put a snood on Hedy Lamarr in *I Take This Woman* and created an international fashion trend. It was the right look for the right time. As millions of women filled the factory and service jobs of their husbands and sons who were fighting overseas, they needed a quick yet flattering way to style their hair. Attached to a hat, the snood was elegant with a suit; worn alone in the factories, it was a practical complement to overalls and jumpsuits.

It can still be a charming, unique accessory. Snoods are frequently worn today with formal riding clothes and can be found in flea markets, well-stocked hair-accessory departments, and equestrian outfitters. Don't feel that you must pair the snood with vintage jackets and dresses. Snoods add original style to contemporary lean silhouettes like slim shifts and tailored pleated pants. You can subtly play up the 1940s heritage with a pair of Bakelite bracelets or ankle-strap platform shoes.

How to Wear a Snood

✿ **white snood**
   blue-and-white-striped T-shirt
   navy cotton sailor pants
   navy ballet flats
   small gold hoop earrings
   red Bakelite bracelet

✿ **black net snood**
   black mid-calf linen tank dress
   black ballet flats
   pearl stud earrings
   pearl cuff bracelet

✿ **black snood**
   white linen shirt
   black pleated pants
   leopard-print flats
   pearl stud earrings
   pearl cuff bracelet

✿ **white snood**

white linen shirt

red-and-white-checked pants

white flats

small antique gold earrings

straw tote bag garnished
   with red cherries

✿ **black crocheted snood** for
   low ponytail

red cashmere turtleneck sweater

gray flannel pants

black belt

black alligator loafers

pearl and jet drop earrings

black melton polo coat or car coat

black faux alligator doctor's
   satchel bag

SOCKS

Socks are the essential accessory. They keep our feet warm and dry and our shoes fresh and clean. We tend to pull them on and take them for granted. What a waste. Socks are a fashion stylist's secret weapon—a quick and easy way to add color, elegance, texture, or humor to an outfit.

There are three types of socks: anklets, athletic, and kneesocks. It's likely that all three are now sitting in your drawers. Which ones you put on depends on how you're feeling, what you're wearing, and where you're going.

Remember shiny patent leather Mary Janes and little white socks sometimes trimmed with lace? These anklets are still around, and can instantly change the mood of your whole outfit. For a romantic look, add them to a pair of ballet flats and a long filmy skirt or dress. Turn your long black straight skirt retro with a pair of white cuffed socks and black loafers. Tired of your tailored pantsuit? Take the edge off with white anklets and a pair of ankle-strapped platform pumps.

True athletic socks look and feel great at any age. Thick and soft, they absorb perspiration and provide cushioning from friction and impact. Usually white, bone, or gray, and often accented with stripes, they are made either singly or in combination of cotton, nylon, Lycra, and wool. Each fabric has its own bene-fits and drawbacks. Cotton is natural, nonirritating, and absorbent, but tends to shrink and lose shape. Adding nylon to a cotton prevents shrinkage, wool adds warmth, and Lycra provides shape. Some athletic socks are lined with terry cloth for extra cushioning and absorbency, while others have additional padding in the heel and toe to reduce impact. The ultimate winter athletic sock contains Gore-Tex to wick away moisture and keep the feet warm and dry when the temperature plummets below freezing.

Bulky athletic socks work best with sneakers, hiking boots, oxfords, and traditional loafers. To avoid a drawer full of unmatchable socks, buy a dozen identical pairs at a time. As natural attrition takes place, you'll still have enough left to find a mate.

Fashion athletic socks add a jaunty accent of color and texture to sportswear. Usually made of 100% cotton (sometimes with a bit of stretchy Lycra in the cuff), they are available in a riot of colors that can include orange, turquoise, and chartreuse. Thick and slouchy, they balance baggy pants and skinny leggings. Fashion athletic sock mimic their hardworking cousins, but do not provide the absorbency and cushioning needed for active sports.

The sagging kneesocks that were part of elementary school now, like us, have grown up, and with the happy addition of Lycra, they stay up. Available in a smorgasbord of colors, fabrics, and patterns and worn with pants, long skirts, and jeans, they deliver personality and polish to an outfit. For example, argyle socks bring a touch of British aristocracy to the hard-working American blue jeans, while cream lace kneesocks add femininity to a white linen pantsuit. In reverse, black lace kneesocks make a gray wool pantsuit provocative.

You will find kneesocks in Lycra, wool, nylon, and silk, and for real luxury, cashmere. As a general rule, lightweight fabrics like silk and Lycra look best with office and party clothes, while thicker weaves like wool and cashmere are great paired with boots and loafers. The ultimate kneesock? Many sock connoisseurs nominate the silky, opaque trouser sock from Wolford, the famous Austrian hosiery manufacturer. But as good as they are, Wolford's share an important problem with a pair of trouser socks from Kmart—they seem to vanish in the laundry.

To protect hosiery from damage and disappearance, toss worn socks in a small, mesh laundry bag hung conveniently in your closet or bathroom. Wash socks in this type of bag in a gentle detergent and dry at the coolest setting. Fold into pairs and keep grouped by color in your drawers. To protect wool socks from moths (even blends with wool are susceptible), drop a few aromatic cedar balls into the hosiery drawers.

H o w   t o   W e a r   S o c k s

✿ pink and cream argyle socks
brown pantsuit
cream sweater
brown suede loafers
gold earrings
soft pink muffler

✿ cream lace thick kneesocks
black twin set
red-and-black buffalo-plaid long skirt
black ballet flats
small antique gold earrings

✿ pale blue opaque kneesocks
pale blue chambray shirt
bone wool crew-neck tied around
    shoulders
camel corduroy jeans
brown suede loafers
pearl stud earrings

✿ black cashmere kneesocks
white shirt
black V-necked cardigan
gray pants
black loafers
jet earrings
strand of pearls

✿ paisley kneesocks
white T-shirt
navy blazer
blue jeans
black loafers
small gold hoop earrings

✿ Mickey Mouse socks
black tuxedo suit
white tuxedo vest worn as a top
black patent leather tuxedo loafers
diamond stud earrings

✿ black ribbed trouser socks
black polo-collared wool or cashmere
    sweater
black-and-white-checked pants
    or skirt
black patent leather loafers
small gold hoop earrings

✿ brown and white ragg athletic socks
white short-sleeved T-shirt
pale pink men's shirt
khaki pants
brown driving shoes
silver earrings
three silver chain-link bracelets

✿ Fair Isle patterned socks
cream turtleneck
brown tweed pants
brown suede loafers
amber earrings
brown leather jacket
brown velvet muffler

✿ white terry-lined crew socks
white terry cloth headband
pale yellow polo shirt
gray sweatshirt
gray sweatpants
white athletic shoes
diamond stud earrings

STRAW HAT

The disarming straw hat has endured for centuries as a wearable symbol of the perfect summer day—long, warm, and sun-soaked. These hats provide a cooling shade that is absurdly flattering, framing your eyes as it seems to erase tiny lines.

There are so many styles to choose from, including floppy Panamas, flat boaters, and ribbon-trimmed Bretons with an upturned brim. Most styles can be accented with a variety of trims. Keep trying hats until you find one that feels good enough to wear all day. If you are over 5 feet 4 inches tall, experiment with larger models such as CARTWHEELS or PANAMAS; smaller frames look wonderful in BOATERS, small PICTURE HATS, or a tight-fitting CLOCHE. Once you find a hat that works, customize it with different ribbon or flower trims.

How to Wear a Straw Hat

✿ **black straw hat**
black short-sleeved
   T-shirt
black linen pants
black Chanel-style flats
pearl stud earrings
pearl and coral bracelet

✿ **natural straw Breton hat**
pink flowered mid-calf
   slip dress
white T-shirt
bone espadrilles

✿ **black straw picture hat**
black and white short silk dress
black 3-inch slingback pumps
mabe pearl earrings
pearl and gold bracelets
black bag on chain

✿ **white straw picture hat**
bikini
flowered short sundress
hot pink thong sandals
light pink canvas tote bag

✿ **gray straw picture hat**
gray and white silk dress
pale gray slingback pumps
small diamond stud earrings
14-inch pearl necklace
gray calf envelope bag

❁ **natural straw boater hat**
  white linen shirt
  white linen walking shorts
  straw ballet flats
  pearl stud earrings

SUNGLASSES

Sunglasses, a seemingly timeless emblem of fame and leisure, were actually developed in the 1930s to reduce high altitude glare for pilots. They were quickly adopted by Hollywood film stars, turning military technology into a fashion statement.

Sizes and shapes have varied from era to era. In the 1950s sunglasses were frequently harlequin-shaped and trimmed with rhinestones. In the 1960s the over-sized glasses of Jacqueline Kennedy and Audrey Hepburn were copied by women of all ages. More recently the fashion has been for tiny dark wire frames in round or octagonal shapes. Not all styles work for every face. The most flattering sunglasses find a balance between current sunglasses style and what looks best with your features. (See section on Eyeglasses for advice on proportions.)

Certain styles have become nonverbal signals. The heavy black-framed Ray-Bans worn by Tom Cruise in *Risky Business* have become a symbol of randy self-confidence; brown tortoiseshell is perceived as a sign of quiet elegance and old money;

small wire rims imply trendy downtown attitude.

Keep in mind that glasses are more than decoration. They can protect both the eyes from irritating glare and the skin around the eyes from the aging rays of the sun.

SUNGLASSES TIP SHEET

- Sage green lenses are calming and casual. Good for everyday wear.
- For strong sunlight, the lenses should be dark enough to completely hide your eyes.
- Mirrored glasses provide more fashion than function.
- Polarized lenses decrease the glare of light reflected off water.
- Gradient lenses that darken as the light becomes stronger work well against snow or highway glare.
- Heather gray lenses show true colors in brilliant sunshine.
- Yellow lenses provide clear vision on hazy days.
- Shatterproof lenses are essential if you wear them to play sports.

How to Wear Sunglasses

✿ **wire-framed aviator sunglasses**
small brown bikini
white sandals
diamond stud earrings
a tube of SPF 15 sunscreen

✿ **black Ray-Ban sunglasses**
white T-shirt
blue jeans
black loafers
small gold hoop earrings

✿ **small round silver-framed sunglasses**
black turtleneck
black pleated pants
Belgian loafers
silver earrings
silver cuff bracelet

THE FIRST SUNGLASSES

The earliest sunglasses were actually developed in the  15th century, not for the sun, but for justice. Chinese judges wore them to hide their expressions during a trial.

✿ **oversized tortoiseshell-framed sunglasses**
blue-and-white-striped long-sleeved T-shirt
white pants
white Keds
small pearl drop earrings

SUSPENDERS

Suspenders are not subtle. A quixotic gender-bending accessory, they become the focus of an outfit. On men they are a symbol of elegant conservatism, on women a sign of puckish originality.

Suspenders on women look best on lean, angular bodies. They are flattering to small-boned silhouettes, adding curves to a small bust. For the best effect, suspenders should be worn with a bit of swagger. The shirt should be full, not tight, and the pants should hang loosely from the suspenders. Carry a pouchy leather satchel rather than a backpack shoulder bag, which adds too many straps.

How to Wear Suspenders

✿ **red suspenders**
white unfitted shirt
blue jeans
white high-heeled sneakers
pearl stud earrings

✿ black and white patterned suspenders

white tuxedo shirt

black pleated pants

black high-top sneakers

diamond stud earrings

pearl wide-cuff bracelet

✿ brown paisley suspenders

bone cashmere crew-neck sweater

khaki pleated pants

brown argyle socks

brown suede loafers

small gold hoop earrings

brown leather satchel bag

✿ yellow and navy regimental stripe suspenders

blue-and-white-striped shirt with
   sleeves rolled up

white pleated pants

white sneakers with blue trim

blue and white scarf tied as an ascot

navy and white canvas tote bag

✿ navy paisley suspenders

cream vintage rayon shirt over
   lace-edged camisole

gray pleated flannel pants

navy socks

brown alligator loafers

pearl stud earrings

leather vintage envelope bag

✿ **black moiré suspenders**
 black snood
 white tuxedo shirt with French cuffs
 black and white pin-striped trousers
 black ribbed trouser socks
 black patent tuxedo loafers
 diamond stud earrings
 black, red, and white
  Mickey Mouse cuff links

✿ **black suspenders with**
 white polka dots
 black velvet headband
 black-and-white-striped shirt with
  white collar and French cuffs
 black pants
 black chunky suede loafers
 pearl stud earrings
 pearl cuff links

t

TAM O' SHANTER

This is the hat that Mary Tyler Moore made famous when she tossed it up into the Minnesota sky. Colorful, perky, soft, and topped with a pom-pom, the Tam is made up of equal parts childlike joy, practical warmth, and centuries of Celtic traditions. Pulled down over the eye, tipped back, or tilted to the side, it is the hat to wear walking through the snow or skating on a pond.

The Tam, named after the hero of a poem by the Scottish poet Robert Burns, is a decidedly casual hat. It is perfect with winter coats and jackets, happy to be stuffed in a pocket when the wearer comes indoors. On a blustery, snowy day there is nothing that warms both the soul and your head like a bright plaid Tam with a pom-pom that wobbles as you walk.

How to Wear a Tam O' Shanter

✿ **navy-and-red-plaid Tam**
  white fishermen's sweater
  blue jeans
  brown hiking boots
  navy peacoat
  yellow wool scarf
  brown backpack

✿ **red-and-blue-plaid Tam**
  off-white cable knit turtleneck
  blue jeans
  navy loafers
  navy paisley socks
  antique gold earrings
  navy peacoat
  off-white cable-knit mittens
  brown shoulder bag

✿ **Black Watch-plaid Tam**
  white fishermen's sweater
  tan gabardine pants
  brown and white oatmeal socks
  brown suede hiking boots
  pearl stud earrings
  brown suede shearling jacket
  navy mittens

TORTOISESHELL

Fashionable since Roman times, tortoiseshell is a popular material for eyeglasses, combs, headbands, and barrettes. In summer, stores frequently offer tortoiseshell earrings and bangles. The mottled brown tones are flattering for all skin and hair combinations, while the lighter blond tortoiseshell looks terrific with red and blond hair.

Natural tortoiseshell comes from the hawksbill turtle, which is protected under the Endangered Species Act of 1973. Practically all of the tortoiseshell accessories made today are made from a plastic substitute often so good that it can only be distinguished from the real thing under a microscope. Vintage pieces of tortoiseshell may well be the real thing.

Tortoiseshell hair ornaments are trim and unobtrusive as they clip back loose strands or casually pull back a ponytail. They work beautifully with sportswear as well as tailored suits and dresses. For dressier occasions, tortoiseshell is too flat and brown.

How to Wear Tortoiseshell

✿ **half-inch tortoiseshell headband**
cranberry crew-neck
cranberry-and-brown-plaid
    pleated pants
paisley socks
brown suede loafers
small gold hoop earrings
gold coin necklace

✿ **tortoiseshell barrettes**
gray cashmere turtleneck sweater
gray flannel trousers
black belt
Fair Isle socks
black Belgian loafers
pearl stud earrings
gold chain bracelets
black Kelly bag

✿ **tortoiseshell sunglasses**
✿ **tortoiseshell cuff bracelet**
brown mid-calf linen shift
brown suede mules
ivory earrings
tan straw bag

✿ **one-inch tortoiseshell headband**
white notched-collar silk shirt
navy jacket
navy skirt
brown suede slingback
    3-inch pumps

pearl and coral earrings
thin gold chain necklace
coral bracelet
brown suede briefcase with small
    brown suede shoulder bag

TOTE BAG

The concept is utterly simple—a big sack with two handle-sized straps to carry it along. There have probably been tote bags ever since a woman first left her cave and went to find berries to bring home for dinner. But it wasn't until the 1960s that totes became a legitimate fashion accessory. In addition to plain canvas and straw, totes now appear in Italian leather or sporting designer names and symbols. Wearing clothing with initials or names other than one's own has mercifully passed, but totes are still a socially approved bag. It is the perfect way of carrying those parts of life that don't fit into a handbag (e.g., run-

ning shoes, bottled water, chew toys, and a spare diaper).

Casual totes in canvas, straw, and cotton are wonderful beach bags and airplane carry-ons. Totes of coated linen, suede, and vinyl are trim and tailored and have zippered side pockets. These are excellent for work and can be stuffed and lugged without mercy. Expect even the best quality tote to show signs of wear and tear, especially at the bottom corners and where handles attach. Enjoy your tote, but don't fall in love. Be prepared to replace it when it wears out.

If you are shorter than 5 feet 4 inches, always check the hanging length of a tote. You don't want to drag it on the ground.

How to Wear a Tote Bag

❁ **straw tote bag**
bathing suit
sandals
sunglasses
small gold hoop earrings
thin gold chain at neck

❁ **black nylon tote bag**
black wool pantsuit
white T-shirt
black sheer trouser socks
black patent leather Belgian loafers
silver earrings
silver chain-link bracelets

✿ **saddle brown leather tote bag**
   white T-shirt
   navy blazer
   khaki pants
   white crew socks
   bone and tan saddle shoes
   gold earrings
   gold chain bracelets

TRILBY

A felt hat similar to but somewhat smaller than the fedora, the trilby was named after the heroine of a play that was enormously popular at the end of the 19th century. Greta Garbo loved this hat and helped make it one of the most

popular styles of the 1930s and '40s. The soft brim and crown can be "played with," molded and tilted it for maximum effect.

(See FEDORA for styling advice.)

TURBAN

This is one of those accessories that goes in and out of fashion. Worn originally by Muslims and Sikh men, it has been the ultimate solution for a bad-hair day for generations of women. Turbans are not shy headgear. Covering most of the head, they become the focus of a look. Some of the most effective contemporary turbans are worn by African-American women who combine ethnic and Western-style clothing. For example, a colorful kente cloth turban is a proud finish to a tan linen shirt and pants.

How to Wear a Turban

❁ **kente cloth turban**
  bone T-shirt
  brown linen drawstring pants
  brown leather mules
  cowrie shell earrings
  wooden bangle bracelets

❁ **red and green woven turban**
  green linen tank dress
  brown leather mules
  small ivory earrings
  straw tote bag

❁ **brown and orange turban**
  burnt orange overalls
  brown mules
  shell earrings
  wide ivory bangle bracelet

THE PATRIOTIC TURBAN

During World War II the turban became a symbol of hardworking women on the home front. The turbaned head was a signal that a woman wasn't spending scarce resources and precious time fussing with her hair. Instead, she kept her hair away from her face to work more effectively at industries essential for the war effort. Cotton and linen turbans were worn during the day, while at night a woman could "glam" up with a velvet or lamé head wrap. When the war ended, the turban vanished, as if by national decree.

❀ **black, yellow, and navy African batik headwrap**

navy wool suit with pants or
   knee-length skirt
navy semi-sheer panty hose
navy leather pumps
tiny gold hoop earrings
pearl necklace
Cartier-style tank wristwatch

TURQUOISE

According to Persian legends, turquoise protects the wearer against snakebites and the Devil's Eye. Helpful—but more to the point as an accessory—its lovely blue hue adds a shot of bright color.

The finest turquoise is the color of the sky on a perfect, warm, sun-drenched day. Veins of discoloration or greenish-yellow tones will lessen the value of the stone. The best turquoise is found in Iran and Iraq, with varying grades mined in Mexico and the American Southwest.

The birthstone of December, turquoise is a favorite stone of Mexican, Arabic, and Native American craftsmen. Perhaps because it comes from sun-soaked climates, it looks wonderful with all warm weather clothing. It's hard to imagine a better look than a white linen shift topped with a string of turquoise beads, or a pair of jeans, white T-shirt, and silver and turquoise belt.

However it is worn, turquoise is deceptively fragile. It is easily scratched and can be discolored by contact with soap, grease, and perspiration. Rings run the greatest risk of damage, while pins are the safest spot for a piece of fine turquoise.

How to Wear Turquoise

✿ **turquoise and silver earrings**
black mid-calf linen tank dress
black linen mules
silver cuff bracelet
black straw tote bag

✿ **turquoise and silver Arabic-style necklace**
black turtleneck sweater
black pants
black suede mules
small silver hoop earrings

✿ **Native American silver and turquoise belt**
gray mid-calf wool sweater dress
black knee-high suede boots
small silver hoop earrings

✿ **gold and turquoise Victorian earrings**
black wool suit
black sheer panty hose
black pumps
Victorian bracelet
black Kelly bag

u

UMBRELLA

For centuries the umbrella was only used by women. Considered a sign of weakness, men had to settle for wearing a hat and getting soaked in the rain. Then a brave and persistent Englishman became determined to make the umbrella respectable for men. James Henway spent the last 30 years of his life popularizing the umbrella. At first he was ridiculed as he carried his umbrella through rainy London streets. By the time he died in 1830, umbrellas were becoming a standard accessory on damp English days for both genders.

Once available only in plain, black fabric, umbrellas have blossomed into different sizes, colors, and patterns. Rather than plain and dark, umbrellas are now a full-fledged accessory, capable of adding personality and style to a rainy day.

Umbrellas are not sized to your body, but they probably should be keyed to height. Before you purchase an umbrella, open it and check out the proportions in a full-length mirror. A too-small umbrella on a tall woman can look comic and leave her soaked, while one that is too massive can make a petite woman look like a mushroom.

Umbrellas, like gloves, seem to have a tendency to disappear into a black hole. Because we tend to forget them in stores, leave them in restaurants, or abandon them in taxis, it is hard to care about an item that seems to vanish at will. Try. A bright yellow umbrella can cheer up the coldest wet day while a jewel-tone umbrella adds color and movement to a dull tan trench coat. If you really like an umbrella, chances are you won't leave it behind.

THE QUEEN'S UMBRELLA

In England, where they take their rainwear seriously, the Rolls-Royce of umbrellas comes from Swaine, Adeney, Brigg and Sons, the umbrella maker by royal warrant to Her Majesty Queen Elizabeth. Each feature is designed for endurance, comfort, and style. The hollow carbon steel ribs provide maximum strength with minimum weight. If a blast of wind flips it out, it flips back effortlessly. The runners, caps, and ferules are made of strong rust-resistant brass. To help the umbrella open and close smoothly, the springs are crafted from nickel silver. With a polished chestnut handle trimmed with a gold-plated collar, this slim umbrella is so elegant it can make you look forward to rainy days.

VEIL

One of the few pieces of clothing that has always been worn exclusively by women, a veil can convey several different messages. Depending on style and color, they can signal either sophisticated seduction or youthful innocence. We wear white veils as a symbol of purity at weddings and black as a sign of mourning.

Whatever the subtext might be, veils are intensely flattering, softening features, blurring faults, and erasing fine lines and wrinkles. Attached to a headband or hat, they can add an enchanting touch of femininity. If you've never worn a veil, start off slowly. Try a short black veil attached to a black velvet headband to add style to a simple black velvet sheath. For a warm summer wedding, try a small cream felt hat with a matching veil as a finish to a cream suit or coatdress. Veils that just cover the nose but not the mouth will allow you to talk and eat without the risk of finding yourself chewing on bits of lace.

How to Wear a Veil

❁ blue felt hat trimmed with
   a **short blue veil**
    red-and-blue-plaid coat

❁ tan velvet hat with a
   bone chin-length veil
   brown pumps
   small pearl drop earrings
   bone cashmere wrap coat
   envelope bag

❁ cream silk hat trimmed
   with **a cream veil**
   cream silk suit
   bone panty hose
   cream and black Chanel-style
    slingbacks
   pearl earrings

❁ black straw boater hat with
   a **short raised black veil**
   black linen dress
   black sheer panty hose
   black patent leather pumps
   pearl and garnet earrings
   pearl necklace

wxyz

WALLET

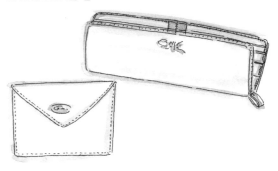

The flat wallet that is found in practically every back pocket and handbag first appeared in the late 19th century when paper money replaced coins as the most common form of currency. It became universal among men during World War I, as servicemen needed something to carry documents such as passports, tickets, and papers of identification.

Contemporary wallets for men are designed to hold just paper and fit invisibly into a pants or jacket pocket. A man's keys and coins can then be stashed in the most convenient pocket. Wallets for women are usually thicker and longer with side pockets for change and keys. Pockets for charge cards and photographs can be found in wallets for both sexes. Available in suede, leather, nylon, and canvas, wallets don't endure as much wear and tear as bags and shoes, but they tend to get soiled from daily handling.

Wallets are a very private accessory and have little visual impact on a look. Some security experts suggest that a woman stay away from a brightly colored wallet, which can be an easy target for pickpockets. If you've ever had your wallet stolen, this may be a way to avoid a repeat loss.

WEDGE HEEL AND PLATFORM SHOES

The wedge-shaped heel began, not as the fanciful inspiration of a designer, but as an ingenious solution to wartime-induced shortages. During World War II, rationing of leather and steel (essential for the support of high heels) forced Salvatore Ferragamo, the master Italian shoemaker, to come up with alternatives using available materials. He fashioned a high chunky heel from cork, attached it to the foot with brightly colored raffia and flax, and created a shoe that was both memorable and patriotic.

Wedge heels, ranging from 1–5 inches in height, clump in and out of fashion, and make a big statement with any outfit. Frequently worn with retro styles, they can be brilliant with a conservative pantsuit. For example, a pair of black suede wedge-heel shoes with white crew socks adds humor and style to tailored gray pants and a jacket.

How to Wear Wedge Heel and Platform Shoes

✪ **pale blue suede wedge-heel sandals**
   pale blue vintage silk and
      lace short slip
   pink vintage beaded sweater
   pearl stud earrings

✪ **red velvet wedge heels**
   black mock turtleneck
   black pleated trousers
   white socks
   red Bakelite bracelets

✪ **navy wedge shoes**
   navy-and-white polka-dot dress
   white crew socks
   pearl stud earrings
   pearl cuff bracelet

✪ **natural straw wedge heels**
   olive green mid-calf linen shift
   amber earrings
   ivory and amber bangle bracelets

✪ **black suede wedge heels**
   cropped cranberry sweater
   black mid-calf knit skirt
   black opaque panty hose
   small pearl drop earrings
   small black nylon backpack

WRISTWATCH

The wristwatch has always been the perfect blend of art and function. It first appeared in the 18th century, when jewelers created tiny exquisite watches that wealthy women wore on a black velvet wristband. At the time wristwatches were considered as female as the petticoat. It took nothing less than trench warfare to put a watch on the male wrist. Crawling along the muddy battlefields during World War I, soldiers found the manly pocket watch dangerously inconvenient. Carried in the pants of their uniform, the large round watches were frequently crushed on the rocks that lined the trenches. Soldiers were often shot by snipers as they sat up to take out their watches to check the time. Officers on both sides began strapping their pocket watches to their wrists. By the time World War I ended and the armies

WRISTWATCH FEATURES

- WATERPROOF: the sealed case blocks the entrance of water, which could rust watch movements.
- QUARTZ CRYSTAL: run by a battery rather than mechanical movements.
- SELF-WINDING: a mechanical watch that rewinds automatically from movement of the wrist.
- JEWELED: gemstone tips on edges of metal movements prevent wear and tear. A watch with 17 jewels is a good competent timepiece, while one with 23 jewels is luxurious and built to last for generations.
- CHRONOGRAPH: a timepiece that includes such features as a perpetual calendar, moon phase repeater, and glowing dials.

demobilized, the wristwatch had become a symbol of macho courage.

There are two basic types of wristwatches—the handmade, usually expen-

sive mechanical watch, and the affordable quartz watch run by a replaceable battery. Both types are produced in dress, business, and sport styles. Prices depend on the quality of materials, workmanship, and the number of specialized features (e.g., date, day, and chimes) built into the design. As a general rule, round-faced watches flatter thin narrow wrists, while square or rectangular shapes work best for a heavier wrist. The fundamental daytime watch can be worn with everything except perhaps a ball gown or bathing suit. It is also nice to have a dainty gold or platinum style for evening wear and a multifeatured chronograph sports watch for outdoor activities.

"Y" NECKLACE

Youthful and dainty, the "Y" necklace is perfect for women who want to wear jewelry but are afraid of being overwhelmed. It combines the face-enhancing charm of earrings with the slimming effect of a pendant necklace. The fresh lightness of this popular piece makes it a favorite with young movie and television stars. It is often called the Friends necklace because of its popularity with the female actors on the hit TV show.

The style adds a hit of color, light, and movement to minimalist clothing styles. A fresh new way to fill in the space

around the neck, it elongates the neck and slims rounded cheeks. For dressy suits and dresses, it can be the small touch of jewelry that enhances a neckline without complicating a silhouette.

How to Wear a "Y" Necklace

❁ **garnet "Y" necklace**
  cream skirt suit
  sheer panty hose
  bone slingback pumps
  small garnet stud earrings

❁ **jet "Y" necklace**
  black cashmere V-necked sweater
  black pleated trousers
  black suede flats
  black pearl stud earrings

✿ **crystal and jet "Y" necklace**
   short black velvet slip dress
   black sheer panty hose
   black high-heeled satin sandals
   diamond stud earrings

✿ **silver chain "Y" necklace with**
   hanging trinket
   white long-sleeved shirt
   blue jeans
   lug-soled desert boots
   tiny silver hoop earrings
   silver rings

✿ **amethyst and pearl "Y" necklace**
   mid-calf lavender linen tank dress
   bone mules
   pearl stud earrings
   small bone crocheted shoulder bag

ZIPPER

Invented at the turn of the century as a new way to close boots, zippers were not an immediate success. The early models tended to rust, and had to be removed from clothing before washing and then sewn back on after the garment had dried. People had to be trained to work them, and zippered garments came with a little instruction manual. It was the innovative designer Elsa Schiaparelli who put zippers on the fashion map. Her landmark collection in the 1930s was described by the *New Yorker* as "dripping with zippers." She put little zippers on pockets, oversized zippers to close a coat, contrasting zippers on a dress, and even used zippers simply as a decoration.

Modern zippers have dual personalities. They are a clothing workhorse, closing up industrial work suits, blue jeans, and leather jackets. Then there is the sensuous side of zippers—an image of languid undressing. To many, obvious zippers are an open invitation to pull.

A new zipper can completely change the attitude of a piece of clothing. A plain black skirt will take on a radically different tone by the addition of a white zipper with a Mickey Mouse charm as a zipper pull. You can add contrasting zippers to pockets and dresses to give an edge to conservative styles.